D1296393

UNCLE NIP

Anne Hall Norris

Library of Congress Number: 2005937294

ISBN 0975518844

Published by: Creekwood Press
            Lakeland, Tennessee
            2005

Cover Photo by Bobby Hall.

Printed in The United States of America.

Dedicated to
Charlotte Bridges
And
Judy Dillinger
(Very Special Friends)

CONTENTS

Uncle Nip

Preface

Printed in bold letters on his rural mailbox was the name FRANK HALL; however, to his nieces, nephews and a host of other relatives and friends, he was "Uncle Nip," and to me he was a very special brother.

Nip acquired the nickname as a child. I don't have personal knowledge of his early years since he was more than 16 years my senior. I was told it was a challenge for our mother to comb his thick, black curly hair when he was a youngster. He cried and squirmed as she fought the tangles, which for some unknown reason, he referred to as "nips." This daily procedure brought taunting from three older brothers who teasingly called him "Nip." The nickname stuck for more than 90 years.

Nip was born October 10, 1913, and formally named Frank Paisley Hall. Aunt Maude, our father's sister, and Uncle Paisley Jones had no children. They told our mother if she would name the baby Paisley, they would make him their heir. She did, but they didn't!

Nip was the fifth child born to our parents, Robert Richard Hall and Anne Alice Weir Hall. Our only sister, Alice, was the oldest of our siblings, followed in birth by Robert, Norris, Adam and Nip, each about 15 months apart. Nip was the baby for almost nine years before two more brothers joined the family. The older of these was John Durley, who died two days after his first birthday. The other, Leslie, was three years older than I. With so many years separating Leslie and me from the other children, we were often referred to as Mama and Daddy's "second crop."

Among special memories of my childhood is one involving my brother Nip. Although we did not have a large dairy, we had a small herd of cows that were milked daily. Part of the milk was poured into a separating machine. As the milk ran through the machine, cream flowed from one spout and skim milk from the other. Mama used skim milk to make cottage cheese, one of the things she sold at the curb market. Most of the milk, however, was sold "whole" to the cheese plant in Olive Branch, Miss. Nip made regular trips to the plant and also took milk for three other families. His first stop was near Capleville School, where "Skinner" always had the milk ready in two or three 10-gallon cans. This was not the case at his next stop. Mrs. Sinks almost never would have finished milking her cows. Although he would threaten to leave without her milk, he never did. About a quarter of a mile before he reached the plant, Nip stopped at Mr. Knolton's dairy for his last pick up. When the dairy plants in Memphis began paying a high price for cream, the Olive Branch trips ended. All our milk then was separated and the cream sold to Clover Farm Dairy in Memphis. "Mammy," our maternal grandmother, had three or four cows and also sent cream to that dairy.

When I was about five years old, Nip took me with him to the cheese plant. At that time Olive Branch was little more than a wide spot on the highway, and the cheese plant no doubt was the main business, except for Brown & Norwell's General Store. After delivering the milk, we went to the store. I still wonder why he did it, with every nickel and dime important to our family, but he bought me a dress with matching panties. To a little girl whose dresses were fashioned from flour sacks, this was the most beautiful outfit imaginable. I can still visualize the bright colors of that dress, and I remember how excited both Nip and I were when we showed it to Mama. I don't know if she was upset over such extravagance, but Nip kept telling her it had cost only a quarter! During those depression years, a quarter was important. Perhaps Mama knew the joy Nip had in buying this for his little sister was even more important. More than 70 years later the memory lingers, warming his sister's heart.

Over the last 30-plus years of Nip's life, he and I had a very close relationship, although separated by more than 200 miles. Between my home in the outskirts of Memphis and his home in Viola, Ark., we communicated by phone calls and weekly letters. Nip filled pages with tales of visits with neighbors, his encounters with various kinds of wildlife, and the trials and tribulations of "old age." Every day brought him new adventures, colorfully detailed in his letters, excerpts of which I am sharing that others may gain insight into the life of this truly wonderful man, lovingly known as Uncle Nip.

Chapter 1
Daddy's Pet

Daddy was a farmer, in a manner of speaking. A few of the 80 acres were planted in cotton and corn, and there was always a vegetable garden. This kept the boys busy most of the year—all except Nip. According to our brothers, Nip was Daddy's pet and did not have to work in the fields. Until Nip was school age, Daddy called him Kitten, probably because he followed in Daddy's footsteps. If he actually was favored, no doubt it was because he was the baby for so many years.

Whether or not our older brothers were jealous, and perhaps rightfully so, they all loved little Nip. When he was with them, they did their best to take good care of him. This brings to mind the tale of "the cat with nine lives." When the boys were quite young, an old tomcat showed up at the house and took residence there. The boys faithfully put out a bowl of milk every morning and soon were on friendly terms with the feline visitor, making a pet of him. One day to their dismay, the cat went into fits, foaming at the mouth and running wildly about the yard. Confident that the cat had rabies, Daddy killed it and the boys watched sorrowfully as it was buried.

The following Sunday evening Daddy and Mama went to a church service, taking Alice but leaving the four boys at home. Although today most parents would not leave children unattended, back then it was considered safe and not uncommon, as long as at least one was old enough to look after the others. Robert always made certain his brothers understood that he, being the oldest, was in charge. They were playing in the yard when a cat appeared. They had heard cats have nine lives and were convinced this was the one Daddy had buried. They were terrified, and Robert knew it was his responsibility to save them all. Not considering that cats can climb trees, Robert instructed his brothers to climb into the big oak tree behind the house. There was one problem—Nip was too little to climb with the others. Not to be defeated, nor to have his little brother be victim of a cat that had come back to life, Robert tied a rope underneath Nip's arms and pulled him up to safety! Mama was horrified to find her baby with his brothers high in the tree. It took some time for the boys to be convinced the dead cat was still dead and the one they saw was just another stray. It also took a while to lower little Nip into Mama's waiting arms. She was sure he was in danger of his very life. She didn't know at that time Nip would have other experiences of greater magnitude at the hands of his brothers.

Robert, nicknamed "Bubba," had an infatuation with airplanes. It was a rarity to see or hear one at that time, especially in the vicinity of the farm. Bubba felt certain if anything as big as an airplane could fly, anything as small as Nip could also fly–if he had wings! Whether the younger ones followed out of respect or fear is an unknown factor, but Bubba convinced them he had it figured out "scientifically." He made a set of wings and attached them to Nip's outstretched arms. Before he was thrown from the top of the barn, Nip was assured all he had to do was flap his arms up and down and he would soar high into the sky. Unfortunately he didn't fly, but he survived.

In those days, so I have been told, Mama and Daddy had a "surrey with a fringe on top," and the lid of the seat could be lifted for a storage area. When they drove the surrey to visit our mother's parents, Mammy and Pa, and Grandmammy, or for a visit with the neighboring Elam family, they usually allowed "Kitten" go with them. There was one time, however, in spite of Nip's tears, his begging was to no avail. He was told he would stay at home with his brothers and sister. The decision certainly was not pleasing to the older boys, whose plans did not include taking care of their little brother. Probably it was Bubba who devised the plan to see that Nip wasn't left at home. With Daddy and Mama still inside the house, they raised the lid of the seat and quickly hid Nip inside the storage box. Keeping his promise to remain quiet, Nip didn't make a sound until they were well on their way. Too far from home to be returned, Nip was rescued from his hiding place and allowed to continue the trip, seated proudly between Mama and Daddy.

It is understandable that as Nip neared his 92nd birthday, he still maintained his house and grounds, mowed and trimmed the grass, kept everything in good repair, and enjoyed using his old wringer washing machine and hanging clothes on the outdoor lines. His brothers gave him a good start!

Chapter 2
Finding His Way

After finishing his first eight grades at Capleville Elementary School, Nip attended Whitehaven High School. His first job after graduation was with Sunshine Dairy, starting in the bottling department and later moving to the stores department, where his duties included checking in the drivers when they returned from their delivery routes. He was appalled at the dishonesty of many of the employees. On the first day in his new position, one of the drivers offered him five dollars as a bribe to check in his bottles twice. This Nip refused to do, making him unpopular with the drivers as many of them had been getting double credit from the previous checker. "They were all crooks," according to Nip, and after one of the drivers robbed the safe, Nip decided two years with the dairy were enough for him.

Nip found his next job in the truck division of International Harvester, where his starting wage was 35 cents an hour. The older employees were making 55 cents an hour and needed all the time they could get. To save money, the manager would give Nip the first available work, causing resentment among the other employees. A tool salesman announced he would be leaving the next day to deliver a car to California. When he asked if anyone would like to accompany him, Nip jumped at the opportunity and thus ended his truck-driving career.

While he didn't find his fortune in California, he certainly had an adventure. He met a young man from South Carolina who had a small repair shop in the heart of Hollywood, about six blocks from Grauman's Chinese Theatre. Money was scarce. There were times when a customer would bring in two cars needing repairs—one to be fixed and the other as payment for the work. The problem was that no one had money to buy the other car. Nip remembered a time when the shop owner traded one of the "payment cars" for a motorcycle, which they both rode.

The Hollywood Ford Agency, a block from the repair shop, needed someone to clean the pit where oil accumulated. This was not easy work because the oil was topped by about a foot of sawdust. Nip volunteered for the job but found that shoveling out the oil-soaked sawdust, hauling it off in the agency's truck, and putting new sawdust in the pit was quite an undertaking.

Opportunity knocked again when the manager of the Western Auto Store offered Nip the job of running his battery shop, which was behind a service station. He soon found himself working both at the battery shop and the service station, with the responsibility of fueling a fleet of sixteen trucks every morning.

Although hating to admit he was homesick, a year in California was enough. Nip returned to Memphis and worked at the airport as a favor to an employee who needed to be off for a month. In June 1937 Nip took a full-time job at Clover Farm Dairy, but the possibility of being self-employed intrigued him. When the opportunity came, he left the dairy and went into partnership with Texaco, becoming the co-owner and operator of a small service station. Money was scarce, however, and Nip could afford to buy gasoline only in increments of 100 gallons. This prevented him from being able to increase his inventory enough to operate the station successfully. When the manager of Clover Farm Dairy asked him to return to work there, promising he would get a salary raise within thirty days, Nip sold the service station. He stayed with the dairy two years, advancing to the position of assistant plant foreman and pasteurizer. He was the highest paid plant employee when he was inducted into the army in 1942.

It was while Nip was with Clover Farm Dairy that he married Hazel. Although he had known her for quite a while, he was "in love" with another young lady. In fact, he was so in love, he proposed marriage. He did not realize until later how blessed he was that she didn't accept his proposal. After being rejected, he stopped at the café where Hazel worked for her sister and brother-in-law. Since he often had been there with his girlfriend, Hazel asked why he was alone. He explained he had asked his girlfriend to marry him, and she had refused. Hazel said the girl must be a fool. Nip asked Hazel what she would have said if he had asked her. She was quick to say she would have accepted. He grinned and asked, "Will you marry me?" Her "Yes" came with no hesitation! They were married November 20, 1939.

On September 1, 1942, with the onset of World War II, Nip was drafted and sent to Camp Berkeley, Texas, for basic training. As a Private First Class, he served as a pharmacist, orderly, and then surgical technician with the 121st Station Hospital in England. He was there when the war ended, and at that time was serving as ambulance driver and deliverer of surgical supplies. While overseas, Nip netted $18.75 monthly, after having $7.50 withheld for insurance and $22 for Hazel's allotment, to which the army added $28. This provided her with $50 a month. Nip deposited $10 every month into a military savings account and used his remaining $8.75 for rations. At that time he was a smoker, with cigarettes costing a nickel a pack. Shortly before his discharge, he wrecked the command car and was flown to the United States with one leg in a cast. He arrived in New York and from there was sent to the Kennedy General Hospital in Memphis. (This facility later became the Veterans' Hospital and presently is part of the University of Memphis. Prior to the opening of the hospital, the street on which it was located was Shotwell. With the opening of the hospital, it was renamed Getwell.)

Nip was discharged from the army on January 20, 1946, and found employment with Armour & Company. Although he liked the job, he was the only non-union employee on the night shift and received numerous threats from union members. This led to his decision to purchase a country store at Brunswick, Tenn. Using the rear of the store as living quarters, he and Hazel operated the store for approximately three years. When approached by someone wanting to rent the store, they made the decision to move back to Memphis and later sold the property.

Settled into a house on Goodland Street, Nip accepted a job managing a Dairy Queen seven days a week, with Hazel assisting him on weekends. He found the days to be long and the work confining. When the pressure became too much, he quit and found employment with Bama Pie Company, working as a route man for about a year. As an hourly-paid employee, he had an extensive delivery route as far as Brunswick, a small town on the outskirts of Memphis. It was on the pie delivery route he found a wallet. From the contents he was able to determine the name and address of the owner, a country preacher who was surprised and more than pleased to have it returned, with the $60 and personal papers intact. Nip refused the offered reward, explaining he had been brought up to live by the principle, "Honesty is the Best Policy."

While still with the Bama Pie Company, Nip stopped by the Dairy Queen, which he had previously operated. The owner was there and persuaded Nip to return as manager, promising he would have an assistant at all times. Although the owner kept his word, Nip still did not like the job. He stayed approximately a year before giving his notice.

Seeing an ad in the local newspaper for a maintenance worker, Nip interviewed with John A. Parish and began employment with his company the following day. Mr. Parrish owned numerous rental properties throughout Memphis. As tenants vacated properties, Nip readied them for the next occupants. He and Mr. Parrish were the same age and enjoyed a close friendship during the several years Nip worked for the company. Although there was no problem with the job, neither Nip nor Hazel liked living in the city. Nip gave a 30-day notice, and they began searching for a house with acreage in Arkansas. Nip, then at age 56, had decided he was "ready to move on to better things."

Many weekends were spent looking at property in rural Arkansas. With the help of a real estate agent, they found a house and acreage they both liked and negotiated to purchase it. They withdrew their earnest money when the owner reneged on his agreed share of the closing costs. And so, the search continued. They had seen an ad for a house and 20 acres three miles north of Viola. The agent was against showing it to them, advising that the property was in such deplorable condition, she felt certain they would not be interested. At their insistence, she finally relented. They found she had not exaggerated. Inside walls were covered with newspapers, painted green. There were holes in the floors, windows broken, and doors hanging by the hinges; however, Nip and Hazel saw the possibility of this becoming their dream home.

Weekends they headed for Arkansas in their 1956 Ford, a six-cylinder, two-door sedan, pulling a rickety trailer loaded with equipment and supplies for cleaning and repairing. Within a short time it became evident a pickup truck was essential. Assuring Hazel he would not spend more than $2,000 (almost their entire savings), Nip bought a new pickup truck for $1,995 from the Hull-Dobbs Ford Agency and sold their car to a friend for $100.

The two continued the weekend work for a year before they moved into the house. During that time, they paneled all the walls, installed ceiling board, covered the floors and replaced windowpanes. The repairs seemed endless, but they enjoyed the work. After taking apart the black, wood-burning cook stove in the kitchen and giving it a thorough scrubbing, they found that most of the external surfaces were white enamel. "Old Betsy," as they affectionately named the stove, soon became the mainstay for both cooking and heating, although a small heater (also wood-burning) was bought for the living room. Out of necessity, one of the first projects was a complete renovation of the bathroom. A load of furnishings was taken on each weekend trip until at last they had turned the forsaken house into a dream home. They moved in with anticipation, looking forward to what were to be their best years. They were not disappointed.

Chapter 3
Adjusting to Rural Life

After having made their house livable, Nip and Hazel's next big project was the monumental task of picking up thousands of rocks that littered not only the back and front yards, but also the area where a vegetable garden would be planted. For months this was part of their daily routine since rocks seemed to spring up overnight. These were stockpiled and later used for the construction of two buildings behind their house. One was used for the storage of firewood. The other was primarily for mowers and other equipment, but also provided additional storage space for firewood. Although many hours of labor were required for construction of these buildings, the cost was minimal. Neighbor Harlan Pope offered free sand from a creek bed on his property adjacent to theirs. With tons of rocks and ample sand, the only expenses were for cement and nails. Tin for the roofs came from the collapsing half of an old barn on their property. The other half of the barn was in good condition, but seldom used as it was too far from the house.

Even after collecting enough rocks for the construction of two buildings, more continued to pop out of the ground overnight. Nip fastened boxes to the lawn mowers for the rocks that had to be picked up to avoid their being hit by the blades. This made grass-cutting a slow, back-aching job, but they each had a mower and they worked together without complaining. As their boxes were filled, rocks were piled along the fences on the east and west sides of their property.

Although the ground was rocky, their garden flourished year after year. The underground cellar, adjoining the garage and workshop, soon was lined with shelves of canned vegetables and fruits. To supplement the few existing fruit trees, they planted others—peach trees, apple trees, cherry trees, and pear trees. They also planted many varieties of nut trees, including pecans, hazelnuts, almonds and English walnuts. Before these became productive, they picked out gallons of black walnuts from trees that towered above the west side of the house. Hickory nuts came from trees in the back woods, and these too were picked out and used in the cakes and pies for which Hazel was famous. Nip designed special freezer racks for storage of her baked goods, which they not only enjoyed themselves, but also shared with family and friends.

As might be expected, it wasn't long until they had a variety of berries under cultivation, including dewberries, blackberries, and raspberries. Nip built more shelves in the cellar for jars of jelly, jam and preserves of every imaginable kind. Within a few years no visitor left without an assortment of Hazel's special treats from the cellar.

To keep the rock buildings stocked with firewood, Nip spent a great deal of time felling trees. Some came from the back of their 20 acres, which was thickly wooded. He also cut trees on adjoining property, getting free firewood while accommodating neighbors who wanted land cleared. The wood was cut in uniform length, ready for "Old Betsy" and the living room heater and stored in neat stacks. Our brother Robert had a passion for cutting wood. When he and wife Loraine visited, the first thing he wanted to do was head for the woods with his chain saw. He and Nip spent many hours together, finding pleasure in work they both enjoyed.

During the early years of their living in Arkansas, I was not able to visit with Nip and

Hazel as often as I would have liked. With the death of my husband Jack in 1970, I found being a full-time employee, taking care of the house and yard, and managing two teenagers at home and a son in college, left little time for trips to Viola. Most of our communication was by mail since they did not have a telephone at that time.

During the next decade, with my children grown and having "flown the coop," I found more time for Arkansas visits. Friends often accompanied me and were charmed by Nip and Hazel and impressed by their comfortable, unstressed style of living. It was expected that we would be guests for at least one meal at a table laden with vegetables from the garden, fresh or frozen depending upon the season, and homemade rolls. Often we enjoyed venison, either roasted or barbecued. (Nip never killed a deer, but neighbors usually kept them supplied with venison.) For dessert, we could depend on being served one of Hazel's special pies or cakes, made with fruits from their own orchard.

One of my Memphis friends, Ellen Walker, claimed Nip as her brother too. She and I, along with our mutual friend Dale Ericson, spent many weekends in Mountain Home, where we enjoyed float fishing and visiting with Nell Hudspeth at the Holiday Inn. We always stopped en route to visit with Nip and Hazel. In 1983 I married Felix Norris, a high school classmate, and traded the girls' company for his; however they continued partaking of the Hall hospitality at every opportunity.

Although I worked with the International Association of Holiday Inns, Inc., until the spring of 1992, Felix and I made many trips to Viola. Nip and Hazel occasionally drove to Memphis—usually for a family reunion, illness of a relative, or a funeral. Hazel's failing eyesight prevented her from writing, but Nip and I became avid "pen pals." Other family members, as well as many friends, looked forward to reading his letters. Their comments encouraged me to share accounts of life on the "Hall 20", gleaning bits from his letters stored in shoeboxes on my closet shelf.

Nip's letters often had accounts of their experiences with "the dogs." Nip and Hazel always were quick to explain the dogs were not their own. Sometimes a neighbor would move away and leave a dog, or a stray one would appear at their door. No doubt each felt it had found "dog heaven." They not only were fed choice table scraps and freshly baked corn bread, but they also dined on wild rabbit, prepared exclusively for their enjoyment. Nip set numerous traps because of the abundance of wild hares that frequented his garden. Neither Nip nor Hazel would eat rabbits, but she cooked them for "the dogs." When fresh supply surpassed demand, rabbits were butchered and stored in one of their two freezers for future cooking.

Most outside chores ceased with cold weather, but Nip and Hazel were never idle. A supply of wood had to be maintained inside the house to keep fires ablaze in the two stoves. The old wringer washing machine and two rinse tubs still were filled with water every Monday. Ironing was done on Tuesdays. All the usual household work continued, and many evenings were spent "picking out nuts." Hundreds of books on shelves Nip built along the living room walls attest to the fact that both enjoyed reading, especially during the winter months.

Most of the information in the following chapters has been gleaned from my brother's letters. Excerpts have been included to share his unique descriptive style of writing.

Chapter 4
Shoe Box Tales

Although the winter months curtailed many of their activities, Nip and Hazel continued to stay busy. In February, 1988, he wrote: "I keep plenty of wood on the back porch so we don't even have to go outside, except that I do take the dogs for a walk every morning, rain or shine, sleet or snow. I have to reset the rabbit traps. I don't need the rabbits, but they have started debarking some of the small apple trees in the orchard. I caught 24 in October and November. I would catch more if I could keep the 'possums out of the traps. One morning I had two and the next day I had another one. There seems to be more of them than rabbits."

Nip wrote they had defrosted both freezers, giving Hazel an opportunity to check the inventory and determine what should be planted in the spring. They still had 20 apple pies, "plenty of rabbits" and "oodles" of black peas.

Their doctor advised them to have flu shots, but they refused. " The last time we took flu shots was about 20 or 25 years ago, and we both came down with the flu. We have never taken them again, so have never had the flu again."

A letter was written on a Monday, when the temperature was below freezing and a light snow was falling. Hazel was doing the regular weekly wash, hanging the clothes inside the house to dry. She would never let anything as inconsequential as 25-degree weather keep her from routine tasks.

"I sure am glad I don't have but 20 acres to pay taxes on–19 acres of 'timber tax' plus one acre. The timber tax is just 5 cents per acre, so we don't have very much of a tax problem." A few weeks later he wrote that they had gone to Salem and paid the taxes. The 18-year-old truck hadn't depreciated as much as he had expected, and their personal property tax was lowered only six cents from the prior year. While there, they bought 100 pounds of seed potatoes, three pounds of onion sets, English peas and green beans. They planned to also plant sweet corn and tomatoes.

Nip had cut a black jack tree and complained about the many limbs that had to be trimmed before they could be cut up for the stoves. "The wood burns good, but is hard to split because of the knots, but I have decided to cut them while I am still young and leave the easy-cutting ones for when I get old!" (He was *only* 75 at that time!)

He asked that I bring a bottle of Ochsner's Solution on my next visit, as none of the pharmacists in his area had heard of it. "The pharmacists nowadays just mostly count out pills and capsules." Although they were not out of the solution, with grass-cutting time coming, he felt they both would be getting a few scrapes and bruises.

"We had turkey-burger steak for dinner today (like hamburger steak except ground turkey). Hazel has mastered the art of making cream pies from scratch—coconut, lemon, chocolate, and so forth. They beat that store-bought pie all hollow." ("All hollow" is an expression with which his sister is not familiar.)

March of 1988 brought a heavy snowfall, but did not prevent Nip from walking the dog every day. Soon the trees were in bloom. The first were the almond, peach, and pear, followed by the apple and cherry trees. When the plum thicket was in full bloom, Nip wrote that it smelled like a perfume factory. He reported the honeybees were busy pollinating, with spring bursting out everywhere. "Soon we will be cutting grass like mad. We get plenty of exercise, we get tired, and we enjoy it."

With Arkansas mandating automobile insurance for a vehicle to be licensed, Nip joined the AARP to check cost on coverage for the truck. He was pleased to find a much lower premium than they had been paying, plus they enjoyed the free magazine.

Because they never allowed hunting on their property, deer, wild turkeys and other game often were seen in the orchard or the yard. Occasionally a deer would walk up to one of the windows, as if to see what was going on inside! In April 1988, Nip wrote, "When I took the dogs for their walk, someone fired a shot back somewhere in Clifton's woods and about a minute later, three deer jumped our fence and ran along the driveway in front of us. Number three was a little one; the other two were grown. There are always poachers. I hope the three were all and the hunter missed. The deer do us a bit of damage, but I don't like people killing them out of season. A deer just knocked down the wire over our raspberries a couple days ago, but that was because I took the streamers off of the wire."

Although Nip trapped rabbits and Hazel cooked them for the dogs, the population never seemed to decrease. He lamented that the English peas were beautiful one day and the following morning almost all were gone. He spent the next day putting a rabbit-proof fence around the entire garden.

May 22, 1988. "Our old big black snake appeared again last week. We haven't seen him in over a year and thought he was dead. I looked out back one morning and saw what looked like a big pole swinging from the gable end of the fix-it shop. On closer look, I saw it was the big snake swinging with his head down toward the ground. A mockingbird was trying to peek his eyes out, and the snake was trying to get a mockingbird dinner. I removed the snake and took him to the east fence row. He is enormous now. I would say well over seven feet. He was over six and a half feet the last time I checked, and he is about two and one half to three inches in diameter. I don't like him being around in the back yard, as Hazel might trip over him or step on him when she is hanging out clothes. Then she might have a heart attack or something.

"I see they are thinking of putting wolves on the endangered species list. It hasn't been too long ago when the wolves were so thick around here that there was a bounty on them. People would kill them and hang them on a tree or fence. We used to sometimes see four or five swinging along the gravel road between here and Highway 62."

In June they were picking raspberries along the road, as well as in their patch. While on a ladder painting the outside of their house, Nip saw a black snake approximately four feet long. He reasoned it was an offspring of the big snake and thought it might climb the ladder. He wondered whether he should jump down or wait and paint the snake white if it ascended, but the snake moved on across the yard. Later Nip saw a mockingbird dive-bombing from a cedar tree and he knew it was after the snake. The next day Hazel called him to the back door, saying there was a snake on the step. "I thought it was a black snake at first, but it was not pure black, just sort of slate color. It must have been poisonous as it kept striking at anything I put close to it, so I killed it. I do not kill black snakes as they are beneficial."

The big news that summer was the installation of a telephone. It was Nip's idea, although his hearing was so bad he could not use it. He felt Hazel should have one in case of an emergency. The nearest phone was at a neighbor's house, about a half-mile away, and Hazel was no longer driving because of her failing eyesight. When making the application for the phone, they were asked if they had ever had one. "Oh, sure," Hazel said. Then she was asked what was their old number. Looking perplexed, she replied, "Well, how can I remember the number? It's been about 20 years since we had a phone." It was three months after they applied before the phone was installed because an underground cable had to be laid from the highway to their house, a distance of more than a mile. Nip said he lost a half-day's work, supervising the job! They were the first in the area to have a private line, but soon others followed.

There was a tragedy that summer. The old black dog they fed daily, while claiming he wasn't theirs, was victim of a fatal accident. They called him repeatedly and when he didn't come to eat, Nip went to the road and found him dead. For the first time in over ten years, they were "dogless" and admitted to missing him.

Good news came the following week when rain fell—the first all summer. The water in the cistern had been nearly depleted and they rejoiced to have water again for the garden. Water from a deep well was piped into the house, but cistern water was used for the yard and garden during the early years of their residence. Eventually the cistern became completely dry.

Two of the four almond trees they planted began producing that summer. This was a surprise to many people, who did not believe almonds could be grown in Arkansas. It seemed everything they planted did well. They picked peaches by the bushel, keeping Hazel busy canning and preserving, but it wasn't long until Nip had cut down several of the peach and apple trees. He said they had too many, but probably it was because Hazel stayed busy making pies, etc., and he had all the yards to mow by himself. At Nip's suggestion, Hazel devised a recipe for pear pies, soon to become one of their favorites. She also made pear pickles and preserves and put pears in the freezer. Nip wrote that they were storing away plenty of fruit, especially peaches and pears. "It's said you should eat what you raise, raise what you eat, and be satisfied with what you have, and we do just that."

By the end of summer both were looking forward to cooler days and less work, although there still was wood to cut for both stoves. "I'm way behind with my wood cutting this year," Nip wrote, "with all this fruit at once. I have plenty of wood on hand, but like to have most of next winter's supply cut before this winter is over. The seasoned wood burns so much better—also doesn't leave as much soot and creosote in the chimneys."

One would think they got enough exercise with all the work they did, but in addition to cutting grass, chopping wood, gardening, canning, and so much more, they also were putting thousands of miles on the exercise bike and rowing machine!

In his letter of September 26, 1988, Nip wrote about a visit from our sister and one of our brothers. "By this time you already know that Norris and Sis were here for a visit Saturday. They seemed to be enjoying themselves, and we sure were glad to see them. They were both feeling fine and Sis looks so good to have had all those treatments. Hazel fitted her out with a wig that was a lot more attractive." (Our sister had lost hair due to her cancer treatments. She was wearing a natural hair wig that was short and straight—her usual hairstyle. Hazel gave her one from her own selection of wigs, all "full and curly.")

"She looked ten years younger with it on. Hazel gave her some wig-wearing talk and told her that wigs were no more than glasses or a hearing aid, and to wear it and be proud of it."

Nip took Norris on a walking tour of the Hall 20 and then demonstrated the new treadmill in their "gym." Hazel told Norris he needed to exercise regularly, but should start off slowly. They thought he was anxious to get back to California where he was living with daughter Jennie Lou and family. "We had turkey meat balls and gravy for dinner, and they thought this was really good."

By early October they were heating the house with both stoves. With less mowing to do, Hazel had more time to bake pies for the freezers. Although squirrels got most of the pecans, they had a bumper crop of black walnuts. After hulling, cracking and picking out all they wanted, Nip took the rest to Hammond Hullers, where they were hulled, weighed, and bought.

A November letter reported Hazel's alarm clock malfunctioned, awakening her at 4:00 a.m. Breakfast was ready 30 minutes later, and they both laughed at getting such an early start. "Speaking of laughing," he wrote, "Hazel was on the rowing machine and I was on the bike, and I wondered if anyone ever actually got one of those bikes up to 40 mph as the speedometer reads. I started really digging to see how fast I could get. Well, I got up to almost 30, about 28 or 29, and about that time, I flung a shoe and almost fell off of the thing. Hazel almost went into hysterics laughing. I now know it is possible to get to 40 mph, but I won't try for it."

As of mid-November, he had cut 14 trees that fall, claiming this to be fun when he had spare time. He always cut at least one big cedar for the next year's kindling. He drained their six lawnmowers and stored them inside the old barn for the winter.

Two dogs from "up on the hill" evidently decided to take up permanent residence with Nip and Hazel. Even though not claiming them as their own dogs, Nip nevertheless cut another hole in the garage door and put down more hay so they could sleep warm. "The two dogs are so jealous that if you pet one and not the other, they will start a fight. We have had to keep teaching them that we will not tolerate any dogfights. The three-leg model steals my wood when I am splitting wood. He will grab a stick off of the pile and run. He has wood scattered all over the yards. We named him Spud because when he first came here just about starved and crippled, Hazel fed him some bread and table scraps, which were mostly potatoes, and he ate everything. We decided since he eats potatoes, Spud would be a good name for him. He sure learned his name quick. All you have to do is say 'Spud' and he comes flying.

"I went out to the shop this morning and I thought there seemed to be some small things missing. I had put five mousetraps in the shop, and found all were missing. I noticed some engine parts also were gone from the work bench, along with a couple lawn mower valves, bolts, and I don't know what all. I started a search and found the cache under the old wardrobe. There was everything you could imagine under it—all five mousetraps, four or five lawn mower sprockets, a paint roller handle, sticks of wood, and so forth, even silverware—of a pattern we don't have, maybe from the top of the hill. I guess it was a raccoon. A few days ago I was fixing to haul up some wood and I raised the hood on the truck and out poured a couple gallons of acorns, nuts and debris. A squirrel had filled all the hollow space on one side of the hood. We sure have the animals around here this year. Must be going to be a real bad winter."

A few weeks later Nip wrote he had set a wire trap and caught the thief that had been carting off so much "stuff." It wasn't a raccoon as he had thought, but a big pack rat.

"We are keeping busy. Hazel cooked up about two gallons of chili for the freezer today and then we decided to make a batch of barbecue sandwich filling for the freezer. It took a half-gallon of chopped onions for the chili and then more for the barbecue."

When 1988 ended, Nip had cut a total of 23 trees during the year and had eaten so much of Hazel's good cooking, including her special chocolate pecan candy, that he vowed to work a little harder in the year ahead to keep off extra weight.

Although the last week of December had brought several inches of snow, Nip had carried in extra wood for the stoves. Hazel found time for sewing, making several shirts for Nip and also clothes for herself. They received a letter from brother Norris and were pleased to hear of the forthcoming wedding, but had no plans to attend. (Norris' daughter Ruth Ann was married to James "Doc" Short in St. Peters, Mo., on January 11. Ruth Ann retired after 20 years in Nigeria as a medical missionary/dental hygienist. It was there she met Doc, a retired dentist from St. Peters, who also served many years in Nigeria. Norris came from Napa, Calif., where he was living with daughter Jennie Lou, Mark and family, to walk down the aisle with Ruth Ann and "give her away." Jennie Lou served as matron-of-honor and all five of their daughters were in the wedding party, as was one of their sons. Also included were two other nephews, Ken Hall, son of Ruth Ann's brother Billy, and Richard Hall, son of her brother Bobby. Ruth Ann was a beautiful bride in a traditional white satin gown. During the reception, the bride and groom changed into wedding attire they had brought from Nigeria and entertained guests with a Nigerian wedding dance. It was a beautiful day and the beginning of a wonderful marriage.)

In January there was news of the unexpected death of John Harris, son of our cousin Weir Harris. Weir was the granddaughter of Auntie Belle Reid, who painted china and wonderful little greeting cards. Auntie Belle was the sister of our maternal grandfather. Cousin Weir was a very special and much-loved lady. Her mother's name was Anne, lovingly dubbed "My Annie" by Weir and so called by kin and friends.

Commenting on the property inherited from our parents, Nip wrote, "We sure hope the old home place gets sold soon. I would like to see everyone get rid of that burden before all the 'oldies' die out. It could get pretty complicated collecting for the taxes from the second generation since they haven't derived any benefits at all from the place—just inherited something to pay out money on year after year. We are sure glad we are out of that. Sis and Franklin were up here one time and Franklin wanted to sell us their part for what they had paid in taxes. I said I would sell mine for that too. Not long after that Norris and Maxine were here and wanted to know if we would sell our part. They wanted it. I don't know why. Anyhow, we were glad to sell and I told him I sure hoped they doubled their money." (For the record, the property was sold in March 1989; however none of the heirs made a fortune on the deal. The 'farm' was inherited when our father died in 1955. County taxes were paid those many years, as were Memphis taxes after the property was taken into the city. All heirs were grateful when a buyer was found.)

Later that month: "We are eating too much, and Hazel's cholesterol is sort of high. She decided to cut out the egg for breakfast. We both have one egg every morning—used to have two, but have been on one for years now. Well, she skipped *one* egg. The next morning she decided that at age 77, it was a little late to bother about the extra weight. I do fully agree. Besides, she isn't much overweight, and we sure do enjoy eating. We have such delicious food all the time."

February was cold and rainy in Viola, but Nip and Hazel stayed warm. They kept a fire in the kitchen stove throughout the frigid weather, with a fan blowing the warm air under the house to prevent the pipes from freezing.

Inside ducts also carried heat from the kitchen stove to other rooms.

The following month Nip decided to have the truck muffler replaced. "The one on it has a couple holes about the size of a half dollar, and it is getting pretty loud. They are free from Western Auto as they are life-time guaranteed. I think I have already gotten three. This month is the truck's birthday. We bought it in March 1970. It has a little over 37,000 miles now and runs as good as it did 19 years ago, except for the muffler."

The peach and almond trees were in full bloom by early spring, and garden work had begun. Early planting included two rows of English peas and three rows of potatoes. Unfortunately, a heavy rain in April washed all the peas out of the ground. Nip salvaged what he could by pushing them back into the mud, but the rabbits ate some before the gap was closed to keep out the bunnies.

Nip had hernia surgery in April, staying overnight at the hospital in Salem. Ethel Lou Brown, owner of property adjoining theirs, offered to drive him home rather than his having to go by ambulance. While waiting for her, he went to the hospital office to pay his bill. "At the office they started all the ruckus about Medicare and so forth. I said I do not want any Medicare. All I want is to pay my bill and go home. In the meantime the nurses and just about everyone had taken up the remark Dr. Arnold had made about my having plenty of money. When they started asking if I really had plenty of money, I said I guess so because I don't seem to go hungry."

Nip reported Ethel Lou drove carefully taking him home from the hospital, going scarcely five miles an hour on the gravel road. He was happy to be back in his own bed and said if he had to hurt, it was much better to hurt at home! It had been an adventure that he hoped to never have again.

Nip was examined by his doctor and dismissed on May 5, with no further appointment until October. Needless to say, he was happy to be driving his truck again and by mid-May he was cutting grass and doing other outdoor chores. Cherries were ripe later in the month, and they picked five gallons over a three-day period. In an effort to keep birds out of the trees, Nip tied 30 "snakes" (strips of cloth) to the limbs and reported this helped a bit, but the birds still got their share of the cherries.

In early June Nip began picking wild raspberries. After Hazel had put 16 quarts in the freezer, she told him to quit picking as they had enough. She froze 29 pints of English peas and declared that freezer space was getting scarce.

Nip wrote, "I guess I will cut down the apple tree just outside the back door this fall. It is loaded with big apples, which are now fully ripe and useless. They are pale green and soft and have such a sour taste, they would make a pig squeal. It was supposed to be a Winesap, but it must have been an experimental freak, crossed with a lemon. I told Hazel they might be good to make vinegar, but we don't need the vinegar."

The garden flourished that summer, giving them more than ample supply of potatoes, onions, corn and other vegetables. Hazel froze 47 pints of corn and 47 pints of lima beans. No need to can blackberries as they still had plenty, but they enjoyed many fresh berry cobblers. Another of Hazel's special desserts was hickory nut pie. They supplemented her desserts with ice cream or ice milk, consuming 32 half-gallons during the hot weather!

From November letters: "The deer season is on now and it is sort of risky to be in the woods, so I guess I will put off cutting a tree for a while. There's no dog now. We heard several shots and suppose someone mistook her for a deer. They shoot anything that moves, and some that don't move. It wasn't really our dog anyway. I do miss her though, and it left us with some dog food on hand; however I have decided what to do with it. I will put out a little every night. It seems we have a night visitor (dog?) that comes to the back door. Hazel throws out a few bits of bread for the birds and overnight it disappears. Could be a wild animal, coyote or something, but I think it is a dog."

The day before Thanksgiving they saw nine wild turkeys "strolling" down the road in front of their house. "The turkey season is on here, and I guess they were trying to decide where to hide."

The year ended with very cold weather, sometimes as low as 14 degrees below zero, but they stayed warm with fires in both stoves. No frozen pipes with the fan blowing warm air under the house and a heater in the cellar.

Nip shared information about past generations of the Hall family. He didn't know how many brothers our daddy had, but recalled when he was two or three years old, he watched Uncle Joe Hall barbecuing a rabbit over the fire in the living room. He remembered Aunt Donie, who thought the water in the drinking bucket was too warm to drink. He felt that some of our family came from the Fisherville area and most all were farmers and "country folks."

During the winter months they cracked and picked out lots of walnuts and hickory nuts. Hazel used the indoor days for baking, trying new recipes for breads, such as cinnamon-prune, cinnamon-raisin, oatmeal and even gumdrop bread. She also made a Japanese fruit pie and a raspberry cobbler. They never lacked for good things to eat. Nip wrote that they took a loaf of cinnamon bread to Ethel Lou (neighbor) and she gave them three-dozen eggs.

By the end of February, they had pedaled a total of 2,377 miles on the exercise bike, and had replaced the original seat. A month later he wrote they had put over 2,500 miles on it, plus over 1,000 miles on the treadmill. The rowing machine had no speedometer, but was the oldest of their "gym equipment."

"I decided I had better get a new muffler for the truck from J.C. Whitney and keep it on hand since Western Auto in Salem went out of business. I bought one from them years and years ago, a life-time guarantee, so I have got free ones ever since and could still get free ones from Western Auto in Mountain

Home. I don't think that would be fair, though, and also it wouldn't be worth the bother to make two trips over there. Sears doesn't handle 'antique or classic' parts. I ordered some other things, including three fan belts, which are the same size as the ones on the big mowers. They called to get further information on the belts. I didn't tell them I was getting them for lawn mowers." (Nip always has believed in being prepared. Maybe because he was a Boy Scout!)

April was a rainy month and Nip no longer was taking his early morning walks. The rain put him behind with outside work, but he managed to transplant 20 walnut trees that had sprung up from nuts buried about the yard by squirrels. He also had most of the garden planted with corn, onions, English peas, collards, green beans, butterpeas and potatoes.

A few weeks later: "We just may get rid of our telephone if we can't get this problem resolved. Starting in February, we have had a long-distance call every month on our telephone bill that, of course, we didn't make. The telephone company says as long as there are party lines in the neighborhood, anyone with a party line can make a call and put it on someone else's bill. We don't have a party line. The telephone company says if we call them each month, they will take it off of our bill and give us a refund. So far they haven't. Hazel called them yesterday and they assured her there was no way they could stop it. Hazel said there was one way—to take the phone out. We'll see what they do next month. In the meantime, I got the telephone directory and went down the line until I found the name of the number called—a doctor in Mountain Home. I wrote him a letter and explained the situation and asked if he had a record of who called his office from Viola in May. Of course he may not even answer, but it is worth a try."

They also were having trouble with their tax bill. They paid the taxes in early March, but in May received another bill. Nip took the paid receipt and cancelled check to the courthouse and got that one straightened out. He said there were about a dozen old ladies supposedly working in the collector's office, but usually one or two were working and the rest wandering around, drinking coffee.

Birds seemed to like living on the Hall property. A barn swallow built a nest over the hood of the truck and raised a family. Nip noted they were not constipated! He had planned to tear down the nest after they left, but before he got around to it, there were five new eggs. "Every morning a whip-o-will comes to the back step and whistles a while, and we even have one big hen turkey that wanders all around the yards."

In his letter of July 4, Nip wrote that although it was supposed to be a holiday, he watered the garden, picked green beans, English peas, blackberries and collard greens and then split some wood. During the spring months he transplanted a couple dozen walnut trees. He felt many of them would die because he had not watered them enough, but said it would not matter. "We will be getting close to 100 years old by the time they are big enough to bear, and I doubt if I will be interested in picking up walnuts at that age.

"We may not have a dog, but Hazel feeds a *Tiger* every night. At least Hazel named him Tiger—a little gray kitten, so wild he won't even come up close until she puts his food out and comes back into the house. If she calls to him, he takes off fast; however if Hazel hasn't put any food out when he arrives, he comes up on the front porch and looks in the window to see what's wrong. Hazel tried putting his food on the front porch, but he knew it was supposed to be out back. She had to take it out back before he would come up."

A few weeks later they still had not tamed Tiger, but he had begun coming earlier every morning and spending the day on the front porch. Nip thought maybe the cat liked to watch TV through the window. When they went into the kitchen, the cat would go to the back door. They also had begun feeding a big white dog that belonged to neighbors, who had two other dogs as well. They felt the big dog didn't get much to eat because he was old and had teeth missing. Nip claimed that when the dog arrived at the back door, he would ask if he wanted breakfast, and the dog would say "woof." He would ask if he wanted bread and would get two woofs. "Then I ask him if he wants gravy on his bread, and he woofs several times. He usually lies on the front porch for about 30 minutes after he eats and then goes home."

A month later, Hazel was running off the dogs with a fly swatter because they were bothering Tiger, the outside cat, and Jennie, the indoor cat. "Jennie came here starved to death and unbelievably poor; didn't know much about eating, just wanted milk and more milk. She learned to eat in a hurry and kept eating until about the second day. Her sides looked like she had swallowed a cantaloupe or a grapefruit." A few weeks later both cats were gone, but Tiger reappeared occasionally. Hazel continued trying to tame him, at first putting his food about two feet from the porch. She then moved it onto the steps, and finally onto the front porch.

"We often see a mama deer and twin babies in the yard, coming close to the house at times. The deer have eaten most of the apples, with the adult picking off the fruit for the little ones."

In mid-September, Nip wrote he had a snake about 3 ½ feet long in the wood yard. He said it was a good snake so he didn't bother it! He definitely believed one should "live and let live."

"We didn't get any 'trick-or treaters' on Halloween. We didn't expect any as there are no kids around here anymore. We just got the candy mostly for us. It is a good excuse for getting candy that we don't need to be eating."

In late fall they picked the last of the apples. Hazel made 25 apples pies—24 for the freezer and one to eat while still warm. The rest of the apples were made into applesauce and apple butter. Nip hulled walnuts, to be "cracked and picked" when he found it too cold for outside work. As long as weather permitted, he cut trees and split wood, always hauling it to the back yard before the beginning of hunting season, not wanting to be mistaken for a deer. Neighbor Ewell Brown brought them a deer ham, which Hazel cooked for the freezer.

Nip wrote he had gotten a pair of "Arobic glasses." He didn't say where he got them, but "they are solid black except for some tiny holes in the 'lens.' They are supposed to just about cure stigmatism, which is mostly why you have to wear prescription glasses. I couldn't believe it when I put them on. I can't read normal printing without glasses, but I can read with them on without glasses. Supposed to wear them only 10 or 15 minutes a day as they sort of put a strain on the eyes. They take all the blur out of the small print. It would be something if they should eliminate the use of glasses."

They cancelled plans to go to Mountain Home in December, deciding it was too cold and they would just wait until spring. It was not too cold, however, for Hazel to do the weekly wash every Monday, even though it meant hanging clothes to dry throughout the house. Tuesday was ironing day and she ironed *everything*, including washcloths and towels, sheets and pillowcases.

Chapter 5
More from the Shoe Boxes

The year 1991 began with three weeks of snow and ice. With new snow tires on the truck and a load of wood for traction, Nip and Hazel managed to continue most of their regular routine. He shoveled a path to the fix-it shop and wood shed and carted stove wood to the front porch, having sealed off the back door.

That year Nip mailed Christmas cards to two people who had died. "I got one card back. The post office had stamped it 'Moved. Left no address.' When you get to be our age, there are a lot of people you used to know that are no longer among us."

From a January letter, "I caught a big pack-rat in the wire trap. I dislike killing, even rats, so I took him down to the push-up, where there is a ground hog den. There is a big hole where he goes in and I just stuck the end of the trap almost in the hole and opened the door. The rat went into the hole. Maybe they made friends or maybe the ground hog eliminated the rat. Yesterday I caught another smaller rat in the same trap. I took that one to the back of the Hall 20 and told him to head for the Missouri line."

To accommodate all the usual 'junk mail,' Nip bought the biggest mailbox he could find. "It's about the size of an egg crate. Two days after I put it up, we got two packages along with all the usual junk mail, and the mailperson got everything into the box." (They referred to their current mailperson as "Sudy Sudy.")

They took advantage of the cold weather to defrost both freezers, which were on the enclosed back porch. With the kitchen door shut, there was no need to hurry. It was frigid on the porch and food from the freezer would not thaw while they worked.

At that time my daughter Janet was attending Memphis State University and was writing a family paper, **"HALL WAYS,"** as a project assignment. Nip was one of her best contributors of articles, usually writing about happenings from his youth. "I thought about writing about the time when we were kids and Robert was building a two-hole outhouse and sawed the end of a rafter off that he was bearing down on and fell from the roof and broke his collar bone. I don't know whether Janet can use what I write, but she can sort it out and discard what she doesn't want. Her paper is getting better all the time."

Spring weather brought blooms to their wild pears, apricots and quinces, as well as forsythia and daffodils. Nip stayed busy spraying fruit trees. He complained that the trees were never all ready for spraying at the same time. "It looks like we will have a bumper crop of all kinds of fruit, and the pecan and walnut trees are loaded with blooms. We hope we don't have a late frost or freeze now."

Keeping everything in good repair was always a priority for Nip and Hazel. He spent hours scraping and painting windows in between the usual chores, such as cutting grass and hauling dead wood. "I have to replace the frames and woodwork on some of the windows; also some of the screens have to be rebuilt. If I ever get the windows finished, we plan to paint the house (maybe). Also the board fence out front looks really cruddy. I may have to go to the sawmill and get some more boards for it." (The joy of country living!)

They drove to Mountain Home (about 30 miles from Viola) to buy paint and a new stepladder. While at the hardware store, they saw a big Yazoo self-propelled lawn mower, a non-compliance commercial model that was exempt from various safety devices on most mowers. It had a 24-inch cut and only one control lever. They thought about it en route home, and although $820 seemed a lot to pay for a mower, they decided it was what they needed. After unloading the paint and ladder, they drove back to Mountain Home and bought the mower. A few weeks later, Nip reported it to be "really good"—just one lever (go) and the throttle. Decals on the mower stated it was for commercial use, exempt from safety regulations.

Hazel put 16 quarts of cherries in the freezer, and in early June they picked plums daily and froze 16 quarts of juice. Although they did not pick dewberries and raspberries, having an ample supply already frozen, they picked blackberries to be canned and frozen. Blackberry cobbler was a favorite.

Both Nip and Hazel had a love of nature. In the middle of summer, he wrote, "Last week we looked out the kitchen window and a mockingbird was dive-bombing a big black snake that wanted to go up the tree and get her babies. I took a broom and herded the snake right through the orchard and out the other end. He wanted to go up every tree he came to in the orchard, but I kept him moving. Sometimes he would strike back at the broom. I told Hazel it was too bad he didn't raise up high enough to hit one of the wires on the electric fence. For several years we have had a couple of squirrels that were into everything, and a couple weeks ago one got electrocuted on the fence. It burned all the fur off of him on the side that was on the ground. The other one must have got a jolt too because we haven't seen a squirrel around here since then." A few weeks later a deer got tangled in the electric fence and broke a wire, however it only gave him a jolt and no serious harm. A skunk tried to cross the fence too, and unfortunately, they had left the kitchen window open. The smell stayed inside and outside the house for days. Nip advised it best to never agitate a skunk!

One July day they watched a buck and a doe eating peaches. It was unusual for a buck to come into the yard during mid-day, even though he sometime stayed in the orchard area while the doe was in the back yard. "They are interesting to watch because they don't swallow the seed. They chew up the peaches and spit out the seed."

It seemed they had a part-time cat—one that came and went as he wished. According to Nip, the cat would eat breakfast and sometimes supper for several days and then would disappear for three or four days. "He was pretty tame until the snake got on the porch while he was there. I swept the snake off of the porch, which the cat appreciated, but I think he has the idea that we keep snakes in the house as he hasn't been inside since then. Hazel propped the storm door open with a wedge, and he promptly batted the wedge out. She propped it open again and he did the same thing again. I don't know whether he thought the door wedge was a snake or just didn't want a snake to come out, or go inside. I think I saw the same black snake in the back yard. I didn't want to step on it, so I got it to move out of the way and up into the honeysuckle bush."

Their country life was filled with many surprises, and his letters were filled with interesting tales. "The other morning when I was getting up, I saw a frog going up the window screen. I watched and he went all the way up and out of sight. After breakfast I went outside and looked, and there he sat on top of the window frame. He stayed up there all day and came down just before dark."

Toward the end of summer Nip removed the electric fence since deer were frequently breaking a wire. The first day after it was removed, they noted 10 deer in the orchard and yard. There were two bucks, two young ones, and the rest were does. A photographer came to their house one day and asked permission to take pictures of the deer. Hazel said he was welcome to make pictures, but no shooting allowed.

A rainy September kept them still mowing grass. They also were spending a lot of time picking and processing pears. Limbs broke from weight of the fruit. "Luckily the deer just love shriveled up pears and don't care much for the good ones. A couple days ago we were watching TV just before dark and a couple of deer were in the front yard. The buck was fascinated with the TV sound. He came and stood at the window listening. He seemed to like the program even if he couldn't see the picture. Hazel put up 15 jars of pear honey and 15 jars of pear jam. Maybe we will get time for pear preserves next week if we can put off some grass cutting."

In the fall and winter months they spent many hours cracking and picking out pecans and walnuts, although the squirrels got a big share of the pecans. They watched television very little because the programs generally were not to their liking and reception was limited.

In December Nip wrote about a new problem. "I have a big, almost pure white skunk that has taken up residence in the garage. He (or she) sleeps in there day times and goes out just about dark. He isn't afraid of me and except for messing things up a bit, doesn't cause any confusion. I can go in and get the truck out or put the truck back, and it doesn't disturb him. I tried every sort of way to keep him out, but no luck. I even put a big 2 x 6 timber across the inside of the doors after he had gone out at night; also put an iron pipe and things across on the outside, but he just tunneled under everything and the next morning was peacefully sleeping in there. I got some deer and gopher repellant and put enough in there that you could smell it everywhere, but he seemed to like the odor! I just decided to let well enough alone and not get him aggravated. He has been with us since some time in November."

As the year drew to a close, Nip gave an update on his visitor. "The skunk has decided to bed down under the hay in the back of the garage. Hazel said I should just remove the hay and run it through the shredder. I don't think much of the idea of tossing hay with a pitchfork while there is a skunk somewhere underneath, so I decided to just let well enough alone. Maybe he will leave next spring. In the meantime if he doesn't bother me, I won't bother him."

Nip started the year 1992 by changing the oil in the pickup truck and giving it a grease job, something he always did himself to ensure it was done correctly. Total mileage at that time: 41,826, much of which was from the days they lived in Memphis and drove to Viola on weekends to work on the house. They defrosted the big freezer and inventoried the contents to determine what should be planted in the garden as soon as the weather permitted. He wrote, "Our neighbor (Walter Dillinger) is running for sheriff this year. We hope he makes it. It would be nice to have the sheriff as a next door neighbor, sort of safer (maybe)."

Bad news came in a March letter. Neighbor Ewell Brown died of a heart attack on February 27 at age 64. He had kept them supplied with venison every year.

Commenting on an article in the Memphis paper about Brunswick, Tenn., Nip wrote that he had known Truman Snowden (featured in the article). "He was postmaster when we were out there, besides operating the Griffin & Snowden store. I used to sometimes hang out the mail when Mr. Crook wanted to be off or something. The mail came in on the morning train, which didn't even slow down for the small towns. If the mail wasn't hung on the rack before you heard the whistle blow for Arlington, you had better get in high gear! The pickup mailbag was filled about equally bottom and top, with a strap around the middle and hung on a post beside the track. The L-shaped supports faced the way the train ran, and from the mail coach there was a steel arm which hit the mail bag a wallop in the middle, and they caught it. In the meantime they threw out the incoming mail, supposedly in the road as they passed. Quite often they missed and the mail landed in the ditch or sometimes a bit farther up in the pit of water beside the track. There were four stores in Brunswick when we were there, five if you counted Ryland Bledsoe's on the other side of the river."

Neighboring property changed hands that spring when Ethel Lou Brown auctioned off part of her land. She kept forty acres adjoining Nip and Hazel's property and said she absolutely would not sell it.

They enjoyed visitors, one being Loyal Foster, retired forest ranger, who occasionally stopped to chat awhile. Another was not so welcome. "I got rid of the skunk, now a ground hog has decided to live in the garage. He dug a pit or hole several feet deep, shoveled out a couple or so bushels of dirt and so forth. I shoveled the dirt right back into the hole. I don't know whether he was in it or not. I haven't checked, but I think I can shovel the dirt back as fast as he can dig it out, and he will give up." He later wrote the ground hog had gone, but deer were frequent visitors and a turkey hen often strolled through the garden.

In most small country communities, cleaning and making necessary repairs at the local cemetery is a regular spring activity. Viola is no exception. "Saturday before last they had a cemetery work day at the Mt. Calm Cemetery and I went. Since I didn't know what they were figuring on, I took a lawnmower, rakes, hoe, shovel, weedeater and all; however all I needed was a shovel. Didn't really need that as some brought two shovels and wheelbarrows. The deal was that the sunken places were to be filled so the mower would go over them. Well, they didn't get a good response and there were five of us old men shoveling dirt. I was the youngest at 78. The other four were 79, 80, 81, and 82. We had one young man who pushed the wheelbarrows about as fast as we loaded them. We had about five or six wheelbarrows, so he always had one or two full when he came back. They had gotten someone to haul in 10 or 12 dump truck loads of rich dirt and dumped it along the back fence, which is now the middle fence as they have doubled the size of the cemetery. We did get one young boy there with a wheelbarrow and a shovel for a while. There were plenty of wives, or other ladies, who raked and burned leaves and got dinner ready. They had enough food to feed about 10 times as many as were there. I think they were expecting a crowd. I wasn't intending to stay for dinner, but they insisted, so I couldn't refuse. We ate at tables back of the Mt. Calm Church. Hazel didn't go because we didn't know the women were going to be there."

Summer months brought long days of tree cutting, stove wood chopping, grass cutting, preserving of vegetables and fruits, both canning and freezing, and the usual washing, ironing and other household chores. Although they enjoyed ice cream (chocolate) every day, they decided to cut back on calories by eating "Jello" instead. They found gelatin packed in 1½ pound packages and bought a supply in all available flavors—strawberry, cherry, lime, lemon and orange; however they evidently found it hard to substitute gelatin dessert for chocolate ice cream. In his next letter he said chocolate ice cream was on sale so they bought four half-gallons.

Nip had an interesting bird-watching report. "We had a brown thrush nest in the cedar tree beside the sidewalk out front and yesterday we saw the babies leave the nest. They were doing a lot of hopping around, trying to get airborne. The grown birds were watching them from the power line and cedar tree. Those babies were sure well fed, as they were so fat and plump, they were bigger around than their mama and dad! I told Hazel they had better learn to fly real fast or either get away from the front yard before Tiger came in or he would have bird supper. We watched them until they disappeared, so I guess they got away safely. Tiger came in hungry, so I guess he didn't eat the birds."

Brother Adam had written to Nip and Hazel, saying that he had been trapping squirrels and taking them to a wooded area where he released them. Nip commented in an August letter: "They say squirrels are good eating, however I don't think I ever ate one, and they look too much like a rat to me. Hershel Brown used to keep them sort of thinned out around here before he died. He liked them, I guess, or maybe he just liked to hunt. I shot a couple one day as they were raiding our peach trees, but sure didn't dress them to cook."

That fall a new item was added to their menu: Elk Burgers. Ethel Lou Brown gave them several frozen packages, three or four pounds each, labeled "hamburger." There were other packages of meat that had not been ground, and also some elk liver. He didn't say whether or not they ate the liver, but they found the "hamburger" quite good when mixed with an equal amount of ground beef. The meat was left from Ewell Brown's last elk hunting trip, probably in Colorado. Ethel Lou never liked elk and after her husband's death, she was ready to get it out of her freezer. Nip chopped the big packages into smaller ones of about a pound each, to be used as needed when mixed with beef. He determined they had enough elk meat "to last a long time."

(Thanks to Nip, I learned more about our maternal grandfather, William Weir. I was only six years old when Pa died, and I remembered little about him other than he raised raspberries.) According to Nip, Pa wasn't a farmer, but was a very good gardener after he retired from the Frisco Railroad. He was a night watchman in the Frisco Yale yards. "He used to tell about how dangerous it was going through Nonconnah bottom to and from work. Pa said it was known as 'Robbers' Roost' and he always carried his gun in his lap through there. He must have been well thought of there, as you probably noticed most of his outbuildings were built of boxcar lumber. Whenever he needed lumber, they would get up a load of old unused or wrecked boxcars and hook a switch engine on it. It would be unloaded at the gap to his place. I helped haul some up in Pa's wagon. I was pretty small then, and I expect I was more in the way than helping, but I got 5 cents a day so I must have helped. One day we went to the woods and got a load of wood. At that time there wasn't a bridge over the ditch at the railroad gap, so we had to go down Democrat Road to get to the back. Pa had a little black dog named Inkie, and when we started back, Inkie started across the road to meet us. Pa yelled 'Go Back' as there was a car coming. Inkie started to go back, and the car killed him. Pa sure was torn up about it because if he hadn't yelled, Inkie would have just come across and followed the wagon.

"There is quite a bit of 'history' about Mammy and Pa's place that I sometimes think about. There used to be a real old couple who lived in a shed out in the garden at the old house. They were called Aunt Kate and Uncle Irby; however they were no kin, just an old homeless couple. I don't remember whether they died there or just moved on to somewhere else. The front bedroom of the old house was Aunt Daisy's room, and nobody else used it. Aunt Daisy and Lynwood would come out every so often and spend a few days—I think mostly when Uncle Bill was out of town. He was vice president of the Missouri-Pacific Railroad and had to travel quite a bit." (Aunt Daisy was our grandmother's half-sister.)

On December 29, 1992, Nip wrote that Hazel seemed to have a cold, or at least a bad cough. (Perhaps this was the first stage of her developing lung cancer.) He mentioned her cold and cough again in his letter of January 18, 1993, saying that they had snow and very frigid weather. He had been bringing in wood to keep plenty on the back porch for the stoves, but had told Hazel to stay inside. Nevertheless, she did the weekly wash, but hung the clothes throughout the house rather than outside. The cold weather and icy roads continued throughout the month, but the sun broke out in February and according to Nip, the groundhog surely saw his shadow! By mid-month, they had nearly 12 inches of snow, topped by a couple inches of ice. The mail "lady" missed making delivery to them several days, but finally got as far as their house before turning back toward the highway. She delivered their mail to the door, checking to see if they were all right.

In every letter Nip expressed concern for brother Buff (Adam) who had heart surgery and spent two months in intensive care before his death on February 12, 1993. He felt part of Hazel's illness was from the stress they both felt, not being able to make the trip to Memphis during that time.

In February Nip wrote, "Hazel's cough seems to be somewhat better. She is on the second hundred cough drops, and her face is much better. She has been up and about all day. She cooked dinner and so forth, and is sure on the mend. You know she is really tough and doesn't let anything get her down. She got up yesterday morning for breakfast, but went back to bed and stayed in bed most of the day. I cooked our dinner, such as it was, and she got up and ate. The medications are working real well, and she is not coughing and wheezing like she was." (At that time he was optimistic that her illness was only a temporary condition and he encouraged her to eat more and build her strength.)

On March 3rd, following a visit to the Salem clinic: "The doctor has determined what ails Hazel. She has a blockage in the artery leading to her heart, on the right side just below her neck. She had no pulse in her right arm. The doctor said it could be remedied by bypass surgery. Hazel said she would not have it. He said he did not recommend it. He gave her some more prescriptions and told her to watch her diet as her cholesterol was pretty high. Hazel asked if this was going to keep her from cutting grass and so forth. Dr. Arnold said absolutely not and not to change her life style, but just stop and rest when she got tired or short of breath. Now that we know what the score is, we can do something about it. We will have to cut out some things we eat—like eggs, and cut down on the pastries, except fruit pies, and cut out the rolls every day."

Soon after that office visit, as Hazel's pain increased, I drove to Viola to take them to the clinic. Dr. Arnold, their physician, had found "something" on her lungs and recommended she go either to the hospital in Jonesboro or to Springfield, Mo. She opted for Jonesboro and was taken there by ambulance. The diagnosis was lung cancer.

Although Nip had signed for Social Security payments when he became eligible, he did not apply for Medicare benefits. Hazel had declined to apply for Social Security after questioning Nip as to whether they had real need for the money. When he said they did not need it at that time, she felt the money to which she was entitled should be left for others who might be in need.

They had no medical insurance. With the help of personnel at the hospital in

Jonesboro, I was able to get Hazel's Social Security benefits started and Medicare applications filed for both of them. In the process, I learned Hazel did not have a copy of her birth certificate and the original had been destroyed in a courthouse fire. In desperation, I phoned a niece near Nashville who went to the Tennessee Department of Vital Statistics and obtained the necessary birth certification. This was faxed to me at the Holiday Inn in Jonesboro. Since two proofs of birth date are required, I drove back to Viola for a copy of their marriage license. With these two documents in hand, I located a notary in the hospital who accompanied me to Hazel's room for her required signature on the application for both Social Security and Medicare benefits. Fortunately some of the benefits were made retroactive, which helped with medical expenses.

Although physicians at the hospital recommended Hazel immediately begin cancer treatments, she did not want to stay in Jonesboro; therefore arrangements were made through Dr. Arnold for her to be treated in Mountain Home. After a hospital bed and other equipment were delivered to their house, along with portable oxygen and a large emergency tank, I returned to Memphis. Felix had been hospitalized and I felt needed at home.

It took Hazel only a very short time to decide the hospital bed was too uncomfortable. Nip dismantled and removed it from her room, putting her own bed back where it had been. She also had him remove the commode chair, which she had no intention of using. A week later the rental company picked up both the bed and chair. With a long connection to the oxygen machine, Hazel was able to move throughout the house. Radiation treatments became routine, with Nip hooking up portable oxygen for the trips to the hospital in Mountain Home. Nurses with Home Health Care began coming three days a week, checking her vital statistics and helping with her personal care.

Nip reported that hospital personnel usually met them with a wheelchair for Hazel, and they experienced other acts of kindness as well. In early April he wrote, "You will probably recall back in November 1990, when I had a flat tire on the way to Cabot and the nice guy changed the tire and all and seemed happy to do it, said 'God bless you.' Well, yesterday on the way back from Mountain Home another tire went out, a right front tire. Going out at 50-plus miles per hour is not very funny! I got stopped safely and off the highway and started to put on the spare. I had raised the hood to get out the jack when I happened to glance down the highway in front and way down there I saw a vehicle stop and his back-up lights came on. He backed all the way to where we were and before I could do anything, he was under the truck, putting the jack in place. As I jacked it up, he got the lug bolts loose, with a better lug wrench than I had (which his wife had brought from their vehicle). He changed the tire and everything, then when I offered to pay him and thanked him, he shook his head and both of them shook hands and said 'God bless you.' Now how do you like that!"

The next week he bought two front tires, having already put new tires on the rear. With the trips to Mountain Home, and Hazel on oxygen, he knew it was important to have good tires. However, after Hazel had a brief stay at the Fulton County Hospital in Salem, the trips to Mountain Home ended. When she was released from the hospital, she decided against further radiation and also cancelled the home nursing service. Her appetite improved and she soon was up and about, making jelly and preserves and yeast rolls. She was again doing the Monday laundry, using the old wringer washing machine on the pack porch!

Responding to a question about an old family acquaintance, Nip wrote, "I remember Billy Stone. He and 'Aunt Nannie' used to go to the curb market. They always had sassafras roots in little bundles for five cents each and a few other things. I don't think they took in enough to pay for the gasoline it took to drive all the way from Germantown. Billy was also our scoutmaster when we were members of the Capleville Boy Scout troop. He was also Sunday School teacher in the Capleville Baptist Church. We were all Baptist at that time except Robert. Sis, Norris, Buff and I were all baptized at the same time in Bullington's lake."

Nip and Hazel's home had become a haven for all kinds of creatures. Deer, raccoons, dogs and even terrapins frequented their garden and yards. Nip shared an experience with a snapping turtle that he encountered in the front yard. As he leaned to pick it up, the turtle jumped about six inches high and landed facing the opposite direction, hissing at Nip. Finally, Nip flipped it into his garden cart, hauled it across the road and dumped it! He also reported that he had seen a "little old stupid snake" in the fix-it shop, and it hid when he tried to put it outside so he just closed the door. The snake was waiting to get out the next morning!

As spring faded into summer and the temperature most days exceeded 100 degrees, Hazel's condition worsened. Nip took over all household chores, including cooking, although it was mostly for himself as Hazel found it difficult to swallow solid food. Pureed fruit, such as Gerber's baby food, supplemented her primary diet of "Sports Shake" (chocolate), V-8 juice and 7-Up. Through the month of August she still resisted taking the prescribed pain medication.

In August the Bridges family, Tom, Charlotte and two young daughters, moved into the house "up the hill" and were to become wonderful neighbors. The only other "close" neighbors were Walter and Judy Dillinger. Neither family was within hollering distance, but their houses were within sight.

By early fall Hazel's pain had intensified significantly. She took the first prescribed pain medication on September 21. Since she could not swallow a capsule, Nip dissolved the contents in water. He stayed inside the house most of the time, leaving only when necessary.

"I have been trying to out-think the groundhog under the house, but I finally decided to give in and conclude he (she?) has won. I believe it is "she" and has a batch of ground piggies under there, as she sure is desperate to get back under when I shut all exits or entrances. She digs deep on every side until she finally gets in. I guess I'll just let her stay. Every time I put more glass-wool insulation in the crawl holes, it all disappears; must make a real warm bed for groundhogs.

October 1993: "Hazel sits in a chair near the phone. She has been unable to lie down in bed very long at a time because she can't breathe in bed. I went upstairs yesterday and got down some extra pillows, and by stacking them four high, she was able to be in bed most of the night."

Although always aware of God's watchful care, they found His presence especially evident during the final weeks of Hazel's life. There was a night when Hazel informed "someone" near her bed that she was cold. Immediately Nip came from another room and covered her with an additional blanket. She asked how he knew to come to her aid. "How could I help but know when someone kept pulling my foot?" he replied. On other occasions she questioned him as to who were the people she had seen in her bedroom— "people" she alone saw.

Knowing the end was near, Nip moved his bed near hers, with only a small nightstand separating them. On the night of October 12, he lay exhausted, yet trying to stay awake as he watched her labored breathing. Because his hearing was very limited, even when wearing two hearing aids, he feared he would not hear if she called to him, so he lay facing her bed. Just past 3:40 a.m. on October 13, a beam from the flashlight he had placed on the nightstand shown on his face, awakening him. Hazel, who had been unable even to speak for three days, had reached for the flashlight and turned it on. Or was it she who did this? The last minutes of her life were spent in his arms. As were her wishes, there was a simple graveside service at Mt. Calm Cemetery. It was conducted by our nephew, Rev. Adam Hall.

So ended a chapter in Nip's life and a new one began—one without his beloved helpmate of 54 years. He was lonely but never alone as he continued living in the knowledge of God's presence.

Chapter 6
A New Beginning

On October 10, 1993, Nip "observed" his 80th birthday. There was no party as this was but a few days before Hazel's death.

The days grew shorter by mid-October, but somehow seemed longer to Nip with only Tiger, the cat, to keep him company. He busied himself chopping wood, keeping the fires going, cleaning closets and donating things no longer needed to a local charity. He picked up ten bushels of walnuts and took them to a huller in Viola. When hulled, they weighed 81 pounds, bringing him $8.10. Although he admitted it was hardly worth the effort, he didn't want them in his yard, and the price was better than the previous year when 81 pounds would have brought only $6.48.

Nip welcomed a visit from niece Sue Utley, who arrived with two Kentucky Fried Chicken dinners and the makings of a big pot of soup. After they had eaten lunch, she gave him a soup-making lesson and filled seven containers of the finished product for his freezer. She was back a few weeks later with her sister Cholly (Virginia) and their husbands, Bob (Utley) and Charles Ray (Irvin). They brought lunch and added more food to Nip's freezer. Tiger, not being accustomed to so much company, stayed outside until they had gone. According to Nip, "He was watching from across the road to see when that strange vehicle left, and then he came right on back into the house."

The October weather stayed good for outside work, although rather cold in the early morning. Nip cut several trees and tried to catch up on stove wood. He didn't want the cat to be cold! "Old Tiger sure enjoys the fire in the living room. He lies on the footstool or hassock, or whatever it is called, when I am reading, writing, or watching television. Every so often he will speak and I answer him or pet him a bit."

Tiger was a greater blessing to Nip than he may have realized, for it gave him purpose beyond simply existing during those long, cold winter months. Nip would drive to Salem over icy roads to buy cat food and make sure there always was a good supply on hand, and special "Tiger treats" as well. While Tiger may not have been a television fan, it didn't seem to disturb his napping. Until that winter the cat had been allowed inside the house only during daytime hours, but that soon changed. "I finally decided to let Tiger just stay inside since the weather is so bad. There is still snow on the ground in shady places, and he is not giving any trouble. He stays in just about 24 hours a day—just goes out long enough to dig a hole and wants right back in. Sleeps all night in the chair over next to the TV. He does use his pan on the back porch at night sometimes. I have informed him that it was for nighttime use and during the daytime, he must go out. So far he seems to understand. He doesn't get out of his chair mornings until I get the fires going and get his breakfast ready." (Very intelligent cat!)

Although at that time Nip wasn't well acquainted with the Dillinger or Bridges families, his nearest neighbors, he had other visitors, including Sondra, the mail deliverer, who often brought his mail to the door in bad weather and checked to be sure he was all right.

Nip always had a good sense of humor. An invitation to a Thanksgiving dinner at Gaston's in Mountain Home came in the mail, addressed to Hazel. In part, it read: "Please fill out and return before November 22 with number in your party and current address if different from above; also phone number." Nip said he filled it out and sent it back. "I put present address as Mt. Calm Cemetery and said the deceased had no phone there, and the number attending would be zero. I thanked them on her behalf"

Nip and Tiger may have been satisfied with their black-and-white TV, but the picture often rolled and had narrowed until it no longer filled the entire screen. The new color set was our early Christmas gift and featured something new to Nip—remote control! He thought the set was great, but Tiger wasn't so sure about it. "When Tiger came in, I had the TV on, and he shot out the door like a bullet! I called him back in and he took off again. I turned the TV off and called him in a third time. This time he came on in and got his supper. While he was eating, I turned the TV on with no sound. He came on around in front of it and cried a little, but I told him it was just another TV, so he decided it was all right. He seems to really like it much better than the old one now. He watches it most of the time and I think he has decided that the people (and animals) are not alive. I do believe that was what scared him at first."

Within a few days after getting the color television, Nip was introduced to the new self-adhesive postage stamps. Sondra, the mail carrier, filled the order he had left in the mailbox and took the stamps to him inside the house. She wanted to be sure he understood they were self-sticking. He used the first of the new stamps to post the letter he was writing to his sister. "I think they will be quite an improvement over the old lick-ums, and more sanitary; also they say they stick better."

Nip spent many winter days sorting through old receipts Hazel had saved. Some were from our mother's purchases, mostly for items bought from Sears, with monthly payments usually less than $5.00. In comparing his current expenses with those incurred before moving to Viola, Nip noted his Memphis phone bill always was $2.00 a month. The Light, Gas and Water bill averaged about $3.50, but occasionally was a bit over $4.00. Apartment rent when they first were married was $4.50 a week. Before they married, Hazel had lived there alone and it was 25 cents less. They rented a very small garage for 25 cents weekly. When they bought a G.E. refrigerator, the landlady intended to increase their rent by 25 cents; however they worked out an arrangement whereby she could put food in the refrigerator instead of charging a rent increase.

Chapter 7
The Unexpected Visitor

On one of the coldest days of winter, with several inches of snow and temperature dipping to near zero at night, an uninvited guest appeared and greeted Nip with a wag of his tail. "A BIG mutt. When I tried to run him off, he would just lie down as if saying for me to go ahead and hit him. I decided he would leave if he didn't get food or water. That didn't work. After five days, I just could not see him lie there and starve, so I went to Viola and got a 25-pound sack of dog food. He is definitely here for good. The only thing is he is just too helpful. When I split wood, he wants to catch every stick I toss onto the pile and takes quite a few off and scatters them around the yard." Once "Mutt" carried off the axe! Nip finally concluded that God simply had given him a new challenge. Perhaps that was true, but with the challenge came years of pleasure and companionship.

Since Nip could not hear over the phone, Hazel had told him to have it taken out after her death, however he decided against that. A small amplifier attached to the receiver worked reasonably well, but he couldn't hear the ring of incoming calls. Cholly and Charles Ray took care of that problem. They bought a big, very loud, outdoor-type bell. Although Charles Ray was not well enough to do the actual work, he supervised as Cholly installed the bell on the living room wall. (It probably could be heard at the barn!) The phone was in Nip's bedroom. Several years later Charlotte Bridges installed a second phone with a built-in amplifier, putting it next to the living room sofa, where it was more convenient. She programmed it so he could phone either of his neighbors, or his sister in Memphis, with the press of a single button. He could and did, often!

Not wanting always to be on the receiving end, Nip recalled that Sondra, the mail deliverer, had enjoyed Hazel's "rice crunchies." He looked up the recipe and made a big batch, put them into a plastic bucket, and went for a visit. Although he later decided he should have added more peanut butter, he said Sondra thought they were delicious.

The days passed slowly and the hours were long during that first winter without his helpmate, but Nip managed to stay busy. When weather permitted he chopped and stacked wood, keeping fires going in both the kitchen and living room stoves. He made "Sue Soup," as he called it, did a lot of reading and letter writing, but it was his new friend Mutt that occupied much of his time. Still young and frisky, Mutt was a challenge to Nip. "He usually won't eat but a couple bites and then starts jumping again. I have to hold him off to put water out for him. Maybe some day I will get him under control."

Mutt's presence was not readily accepted by Tiger, who was accustomed to getting Nip's full attention. Nip wondered why Tiger had begun staying away so much, sometimes overnight, until he caught Mutt chasing him out of the yard and down the road. "I was waiting for him with a limb about six feet long and I beat the fire out of him all the way around the house and into his dog house. I told him if he ever chased the cat again I was going to beat him to a pulp. This evening he came around to the front yard and lay down beside the walk. I promptly got the broom and beat the stuffing out of him. I told him he would have to stay out back because he chased cats. I will not let him run off Tiger."

Nip had hernia surgery the last of March 1994. Both the operation and recovery time were difficult for him, but he claimed the tests and procedures before the surgery were the worst part. He "weathered the storm" well and within a few weeks was doing yard work again.

Following his doctor's recommendation, he visited the VA office in Salem and applied for medical benefits. Based on his medical records, approval seemed imminent. In early July he was notified to report to the regional VA office in Poplar Bluff, Missouri, for complete examination by both VA doctors and several independent physicians. I took him since this necessitated an overnight trip. Other than when he was in the army and the nights he was in the hospital for hernia surgery, that was the only time Nip had slept away from home since he and Hazel married. He did fine, however, except for developing a terrific headache.

As summer weather set in, so did a new problem. Tiger evidently got into a fight on one of his nightly wanderings and came back with scrapes and bruises and a large wound on one hip. It seemed to Nip that the wound got larger, rather than healing. Tiger stayed close to the house, most of the time indoors, as the wound continued to ooze for many days. To protect the couch and other furniture, including a bed in the back bedroom where Tiger liked to sleep, Nip covered surfaces with newspapers. He reported, "Here is the funny part, if there is such. He broke himself of sleeping on the bed.

He woke up and was stuck to the paper. I was in the living room and he came through faster than I ever saw a cat run, with a double page of newspaper stuck to him. He made about four or five trips at lightning speed to the back door, then back to the front door. I tried to step on the paper as he came through, but he was too fast. I finally got the front door opened while he was headed the other way. In the meantime, the paper caught on the living room stove on the final round and he shot out the front door. This was in the morning and he got back just before I went to bed that evening. He hasn't been in the back bedroom since."

A few days after Tiger's run with the newspapers, Nip heard Mutt barking "like crazy" in the back yard near his doghouse. "His hackles were all bristled up on his back and he seemed to be scared of something. I went out and took a look and didn't see anything and started to go back into the house. Then I saw what it was. A big black snake, about six-feet long, had climbed up the wall and was draped around some wire and junk I had hanging there. I prodded him and he moved off and through the wood blocks and on down the hill."

Nip worried that Tiger might have died since he disappeared for several days following his battle with the newspaper, however in a few days there was a further report. "Tiger is back. He came back yesterday afternoon about 3:00 p.m. I happened to look out the front door and he was taking a nap in the sun, hot as it was. I asked him if he wanted in. He said 'yaow, meow' or something and closed his eyes again, so I said 'suit yourself.' About 15 minutes later I opened the door and asked him again. He got up and shot through the door like a bullet, never slowed down, went straight back to the storage space in the hall and went back to sleep, or so I thought. I went into the kitchen and was going to get a snack. He was there before I hardly got there, whining for his food. I fed him and he ate a hardy meal and went back to sleep. I went to pick up his dishes and he heard me and came out of there fast and said 'don't touch them. I am not through eating,' so I left them until he ate some more and went back to sleep. This was repeated a couple more times before I finally got the dishes up off of the floor. He is sure in bad shape. I don't see how he can make it, but as you said, cats have nine lives."

Some people may have thought Nip's grocery shopping a bit unusual since he bought as much for Tiger and Mutt as for himself. For example, on one shopping trip he bought two five-quart buckets of chocolate ice cream (on sale for $2.99), 48 cans of Sprite (good in hot weather), 2 sacks of dog food, 15 cans of cat food, 6 loaves of bread, and a few other items.

Letters from Nip always contained reports on his animals. "Tiger is crazy and Mutt is weird. Mutt is the only boy dog I have ever seen that doesn't heist his leg to pee! Tiger, I guess, has sort of lost his mind. He comes in and eats a few bites, then jumps like something has booted him, and runs around to the dining room or kitchen. I guess his brain is shot. He zooms about and won't eat unless I hold my hand on him or rub him. These animals are really a challenge." He often complained that Mutt got in his way when cutting trees as the dog seemed to think he should catch them as they fell. Nip worried that one would fall on Mutt.

About two months after our trip to Poplar Bluff for his medical examination, Nip learned why he had developed such a severe headache while there. He had chills and fever after getting home, and his headaches worsened. When aspirin had no effect, he realized his condition was serious and went to the clinic in Salem. The doctor found Nip's blood pressure somewhat elevated and his fever at 102°. He was given two shots and a prescription and told to return the next day.

Within a week he was feeling much better, but it was yet another week before he found the culprit that had caused his illness.

After getting his strength back to some degree, Nip decided to cut the grass on what he called "the east 40." He began mowing below the old barn, working his way toward the house. When he had mowed as far as the ditch where the drainage ran from his septic tank, he noticed the ground was dry. Normally it would be wet about half way down the hill from where the flow began. Since it would have taken two to three weeks for the ground to become completely dry, he knew something was wrong. Using his clean-out tape, he found the line dry all the way back to the septic tank. That meant the tank had a big leak, and he surmised the drainage evidently was going directly into his well, contaminating the water. He called seven septic tank companies before finding one available to put in a new tank and was told it would be several weeks before the work could be done. He was told to boil all water from his well or use bottled water, which he did. He also discarded all ice cubes and everything that had well water in it, such as jugs of orange juice. To be on the safe side, he threw out 15 cartons of frozen peaches and syrups he had spent many hours preparing.

Not wanting to wait for the man who had advised it would be several weeks before he could put in a new tank, Nip phoned still another company. It was on a Friday afternoon, and Nip was relieved when told they could be there Monday morning. Heavy rains delayed the actual work a few days, but equipment was brought in and plans made to install the tank near the road, with soakage lines running primarily in a northeast direction. A few days later the new tank and lines had been installed, and the old tank pumped out, washed, broken into pieces and covered with dirt. Then Nip tackled the job of loading piles of loose dirt and rocks into his cart and hauling them out of the yard.

Nip soon found getting his water tested was not a simple job. The Health Department in Salem furnished a "how to" kit for the water sample, including a sterile bottle and mailing carton, to be sent to Little Rock. To get a pure sample, even the faucet had to be sterilized. A few days after he had followed all the instructions and mailed the specimen, a notice came from the Health Department. "Water sample rejected. No fee enclosed." Since he had not been told there was a charge, he phoned to see if he could mail a check and get the report. No such luck. The sample had been discarded. He got another kit and went through the entire procedure again. The report came within a few days. "Water polluted." He was advised to wait a few days before taking another sample. In the meantime, he continued putting decontaminating chemicals into the well and drinking only bottled or boiled water and cans of Sprite or Pepsi. Third sample: "Improved, but still unsafe for consumption."

Ticks were an on-going problem, especially during the summer months. Every night, after being outside, Nip had to examine his body and clothing for the little pests and usually would find several. Most of them he could remove, but occasionally he would have to ask one of the neighbors to help if the ticks were out of reach on his shoulders or back. He soon learned his sister would not venture out into the yard when she came to visit, especially after learning he had killed two rattlesnakes and several copperheads.

For several months Nip tried to find someone to replace the shingles on his roof. In the meantime, he made a funnel from a large sheet of plastic to direct rainwater through a hole in the roof into a hanging bucket on his back porch. As long as he remembered to empty the bucket, his "invention" kept the porch floor dry. He was concerned that the fall rains would begin before he was able to get a new roof, but fortunately, the job was completed just in time.

As if to counter the expenses involved with the septic tank and new roof, Nip was notified by the Department of Veterans Affairs he had been approved for a pension and would be receiving monthly checks. Processing had taken four months, but payment for those months was included in the first check. This was a considerable boost to his bank account as expenses for the septic tank and new roof totaled more than $4,000.

Much to Nip's dismay, his dog disappeared about the time the new roof was completed. When Mutt limped home after several days away, it was evident he had been shot and one leg badly wounded. In talking with neighbors Walter Dillinger and son Marty, Nip learned one of their dogs also had been shot and did not survive. Having worked with a veterinarian, Marty examined Mutt and felt it doubtful he would live. He said if Mutt were taken to a veterinarian, the leg probably would be amputated at the hip joint. Together they cleaned the wounds on the leg and hip with an antiseptic solution and Nip continued to medicate the area twice daily. Within a few weeks Mutt was well on his way to recovery, although walking on three legs and swinging the injured one.

As the days grew shorter with the coming winter, Nip became better acquainted with the Dillinger and Bridges families, often sharing fruit from his orchard. His first meal of many with the Dillingers was on Thanksgiving Day, when Marty appeared at Nip's door, saying his mother had sent him to get Mr. Hall. Over the years the Dillingers were the essence of what a "good neighbor" should be, accepting him as though he were a member of their family. The same was true of Charlotte and Tom Bridges, whose many acts of kindness helped Nip through those difficult years after Hazel's death.

As Mutt recuperated, he began straying farther from the yard, often dragging back junk of various kinds. Nip wrote, "I took the garbage out to the garden and in his play yard I noticed a leather dog collar with a brass nameplate. I picked it up and saw it had Walter Dillinger's name and address on it. I told Mutt he was a grave robber and ought to be punished. He didn't look a bit remorseful. I wonder where he gets some of the junk he brings up. He has a lot of checkerdy (sic) woven cloth all over the front, side and back yards. It looks like Arafat's headpiece, however I don't think it could be because on TV Arafat seems to still be wearing his."

Nip was surprised on Christmas morning when Charlotte Bridges appeared at his door with a loaf of freshly baked bread and an armload of fruit, candy, cookies and other gifts. He had been invited to the Dillingers' home and spent most of the day there, meeting dozens of their relatives and enjoying a big holiday meal. To his surprise, there were presents for him under the Dillingers' Christmas tree and he went home with an assortment of pie, cake and other delectable foods.

So ended 1994, an eventful year during which Nip not only had surgery and other medical problems, but also one in which he dealt with a faulty septic tank, leaky roof, Tiger's weird behavior and Mutt's near-death experience. Best of all, it was the year Nip got to truly know the Bridges and Dillinger families, his wonderful neighbors who became close friends.

Chapter 8
New Year, Old Problems

Old Man Winter sent sub-freezing temperatures to start the year 1995, and with the frigid weather came repeat challenges for Nip. The first was a fourth attempt to get a "safe" report on his well water. On the 3rd day of January he mailed another sample to the Health Department in Little Rock. He was puzzled, but pleased, that postage was only $2.70. All previous samples, same size and weight, had been $5.80. His comments: "Postage has gone up, so I pay less. Things sure are screwed up these days, like I get a cost of living raise, so I get less money. I sure am not going to try to figure these things out." A week later he received the test results. Water safe!

An ice storm hit later that week, with overnight temperature dropping to 10°. As the sun rose and began melting ice on the roof, a puddle began forming in front of the larger of the two refrigerators on Nip's back porch. Soon what started as a small drip had become a steady stream, no longer in one spot but across half of the ceiling. He phoned the roofing company even though realizing repair work would not be done until there was a thaw in the weather. Since everything on his porch was getting wet, he had to take temporary measures.

"I went into the attic and got a big tarp and swung it from wall to wall and over to the middle of the porch, sloping down about even with the kitchen door, and let it sag enough to funnel the water to the center and into a bucket on the floor. It was nearly noon before I got all the water mopped up and things sort of under control. Then I happened to notice water also was leaking around the light fixture, so I called the roofing company again. I told Mrs. Harlow (owner's wife) to put me on the urgent priority list as the roof was leaking so bad it was coming in around the light fixture and could cause a short and a fire. In the meantime, I went upstairs and covered the fixture with a piece of plastic. This leak makes me almost wish I hadn't got this new roof. I think there is not enough pitch for shingles on that back porch, but I am not going to give my opinion on that. It is Mr. Harlow's problem. In the meantime, I have some wet wood on the back porch. Luckily I caught it before much got wet. I am pretty sure that the water is running back under the shingles as the coating of ice melts from the heat inside. The roof is a solid sheet of ice, or was, but again that is his problem. I would have put roll roofing on that almost-flat porch roof if it were me."

Cold weather limited Nip's outdoor activities, except for bringing wood inside from the sheds. He kept fires in both stoves, which entailed his having to get out of bed several times during the night to add wood. Sometimes when it was extremely cold, he sat in the kitchen all night to tend the fire.

As had been Hazel's routine, Nip continued filling the washing machine and rinse tubs every Monday morning for the weekly laundry. If weather conditions made it prohibitive to use outside clotheslines, everything was dried inside the house. Many daylight hours were spent reading, writing letters, or picking out pecans and walnuts. While Nip never became interested in soap operas, he watched television for weather reports and news, and enjoyed a few regular shows. Although not exactly proficient in the kitchen, he often cooked dried peas or beans, seasoned with ham, and satisfied his "sweet tooth" with rice crispy candy, which he enjoyed both making and eating. It was taking care of Mutt and Tiger, however, that occupied much of his time.

"I guess I am the only one to get slugged in the back of the head by a dog. When I went outside to empty Tiger's litter pan, Mutt was raising Cain with his junk. Somehow he got a gallon bucket tangled up with some of that old rug he has been shredding. While I had my back turned, he made a wild swing with that piece of rug with the bucket on the end of it, and the bucket hit me on the back of the head. It didn't really hurt, but it sure took me by surprise. At first I didn't know what happened. You never can tell what that dog will do next.

"Tiger wanted out, but didn't quite get out of the door and stopped and started backing up. I looked out to see what was the matter and then I told Tiger I didn't blame him for not wanting to go out there. There was some varmint on the walk and it was bigger than Tiger, but I couldn't tell what it was. All I could see was a big row of teeth, so I went out to get a closer look. It was a cow head Mutt had dug up and left in the middle of the walk. I threw it into his junkyard and told Tiger I had killed the varmint and it was safe now. He finally went on out, but he really was on the alert until he got safely past the walk."

Walter Dillinger asked Nip if he would object to the replacement of the barbed wire fence between their property and his. Nip said he not only had no objection, he would be glad to pay half the expense. His offer was not accepted as Marty Dillinger kept cattle on their property and felt it well worth his time and expense. The better Nip became acquainted with his neighbors, the more he appreciated both the Dillinger and Bridges families. He felt especially blessed when Charlotte Bridges learned how much he liked bread and began keeping him supplied with loaves from her kitchen. It was not unusual for her also to bring a pot of beans.

Funerals in rural Arkansas can be quite different from those Nip attended before moving to Viola. He learned this when he attended the service for Ethel Lou Brown's brother. He knew nothing about the death or arrangements until she called a few hours before the service. He hurriedly drove to Salem and ordered flowers, then rushed back home to dress appropriately, or so he thought. "I really did not fit in that crowd. I put on a suit and nobody else was dressed up. Nearly everyone had on work clothes, jeans and work shirts, no ties or anything. The only ones wearing a coat were Van (Ethel Lou's son), who conducted the service, and the funeral directors. Even the pall bearers were in shirt sleeves."

There may be many advantages to country living, but there are problems as well. Nip seemed to have more than his share within a short period of time. Before the end of February his hot water tank had sprung a leak. "I took the cover off the bottom unit and saw where it was leaking. I got a wrench and tried tightening the bolts, but this made it worse. I cut off the water and got a hose and ran it out the front door to drain the tank. About an hour later, it was still running, so I decided I would see if the drain faucet was fully opened. This was made of plastic and when I started to turn it a little more, the whole thing came off and I really had a flood. By this time, the water was running cold as I had pulled the switch. This told me the cut-off valve wasn't working and water was still coming into the tank. The only thing left to do was pull the switch on the well and let the water all run out. I took the pipe loose at the top of the tank so there was no pressure and just fought it. I could only get a small pan under the drain as it was about four inches from the floor. I got a couple of five-gallon buckets and filled them, pan by pan. Then I poked a rag in the hole until I could empty the buckets into the commode. By the time I had gotten all the water out and had capped the pipe so I could have cold water, it was getting really late. I mopped up the water as best I could, took out the water tank, and looked at the clock. It was almost midnight, about 11:30 p.m., and I hadn't had time to eat supper or anything. I said well, I will just make a cup of coffee and eat a sandwich. Murphy's Law! If anything else can happen, it will! I picked up the teakettle and discovered water all over the stove. Leaking kettle. I heated a little water in a pan, made a cup of coffee, and fixed a cheese sandwich. Then I sat down and took three calm-tabs and started laughing. Never a dull moment. Later I looked at the bottom of the teakettle and it was dry. I have used it ever since then, so it must not have had a leak, but I can't figure where the water came from."

Nip went to hardware stores in Viola, Salem and Mountain Home but could not find a replacement tank the exact size as the old one. He settled on a shorter tank and put it on a five-inch platform so that he would not have to change all the pipes. This involved a full day's work, but he took his time and stopped for both lunch and supper. It was evident there was no danger of his running out of something to do!

When cold or rainy weather prohibited outdoor work, Nip often would "fire up Old Betsy" and spend a day cooking pasta, beans, collard greens, corn, and other vegetables. These would be frozen in plastic containers. Later when he wanted to eat any of this, he simply took the container from his freezer and dropped it into Old Betsy's reservoir of hot water. In about an hour's time, it not only was thawed, but also was warm and ready for the table.

Nip got a bit of a scare in early spring when he mowed the grass for the first time that season. The grass, having died during the winter, was dry and dusty and he felt a little itchy when he finished. When he went into the bathroom and took off his shirt, he was shocked by what he saw in the mirror. His chest and abdomen were covered with brilliant red spots! "I said 'Great Day in the Morning! What is this? Maybe Scarlet Fever or something!' I made a beeline for the phone. I saw it was too late to get to the clinic as it was 4:45 and they close at 5:00 unless they are overloaded, but I called them anyhow and asked how long they would be open. She said they were practically closed and had only three more patients. I told her what my problem was, and she said to just hold on and she would let me talk to Dr. Arnold. Every now and then she would come back on the line and ask if I was still there. Finally Dr. Griffin Arnold came on the line and I told him how I was broke out. He said I had an allergy and asked if I had any Benadryl. I said yes. He said to use that and come into the clinic first thing in the morning. I said O.K. I had a tube of Benadryl cream, which didn't go far on all that rash. By the time I went to bed it had gone all the way down to my feet. I was really covered!"

The next morning his face too was spotted. He went to the clinic early, wanting to be the first patient. The doctor examined him and said he apparently had breathed in a lot of pollen, probably oak. He gave him a shot in the rear and said that should cure it. He asked if Nip had taken the Benadryl. That's when Nip learned the doctor had meant for him to take Benadryl capsules! He stopped at the drug store and bought some before going home. Tim, the pharmacist, advised him to take a tablet every four hours until the rash began losing color. In a few days the spots were gone, but thereafter he kept Benadryl (or the generic) in his medicine cabinet.

When one lives alone and hears voices in another room, it can be a rather frightening experience as Nip related. "I really got a jolt this morning. I had just got up and started to the kitchen when I distinctly heard someone say 'Good Morning' and then said something else. I looked out the front door. Nobody. I turned up my hearing aid a bit louder, and sure enough, someone said, 'We may get a bit of sunshine by noon today.' I looked over at the TV. It was off. Then I walked over real close and about that time music started playing. I located it. The radio-clock. I have never had the radio on, but last night before I went to bed I had reset the clock because it had been blinking from when the power went off. When I set it, I had gotten the dial turned just a wee bit past the 'off' toward 'radio' and somehow it decided to tune in. I guess maybe vibration from me walking across the room. I moved the dial back to 'off' and it shut up."

Nip always has considered his animals to be intelligent and compassionate. Writing about Mutt, he noted: "It is remarkable how he looks after Tiger. They were both on the front porch asleep when a stray dog stopped in the road. Mutt got up and stood between Tiger and the stray dog. Tiger knows that Mutt has a sore foot and stayed near him all day yesterday. He slept under the honeysuckle bush in the back yard all yesterday morning because Mutt was back there. Then in the afternoon Mutt slept in the wood yard, so Tiger got up onto the rack where I cut poles and stayed there all afternoon to be close to Mutt."

Without Hazel, keeping the grass cut was more time-consuming and a bigger job than Nip cared to handle with his old "walking mowers" so he bought a "riding mower." Everything was going great until one afternoon when he was mowing and rain began. He stopped to take clothes off of the lines before they got wet and then decided to fill the gas tank on the mower before putting it away. To his dismay, he couldn't start it. After trying everything he could think of, he had to give up. Early the next morning he phoned Aid Hardware, where he had bought the mower. Mr. King, who had sold him the mower, came within an hour and gave it his best effort. Finally he admitted he was baffled. With Nip's help, he loaded the mower into his truck and said someone smarter than he would have to look at it. Two hours later, he was back with the problem solved. A walnut! While Nip had been taking the clothes inside, a squirrel evidently had found a good place to store a walnut. It was completely out of sight, but one of the built-in safety devices prevented a lever from going back far enough to start the mower. Nip complained about the required safety devices. "If you get off the seat, or even raise up a bit, it cuts the motor off. This is in case you fall off or something. Also they won't start unless you have the brake pedal pressed all the way down. Every time I see a rock or something, I have to cut the motor off, pick up the rock, get back on, and start up again. It will really cut a lot of grass in a hurry though, and it is sort of fun to operate." Not long after that, Nip bought a bright red cart to hitch onto the mower. He used the cart instead of his truck when hauling wood. More fun!

Chapter 9
Two-Way Conversations

Nip communicated with God on a daily basis, not once or twice but many times throughout the day. Most of the time he did the talking, offering praise and concerns and giving thanks for his many blessings. He often received specific answers.

On a cloudy summer day with moderately hot temperature, Nip found the weather favorable for mowing grass. After an hour on the riding mower, he stopped to refuel and have an ice cream break. He rested a short while and decided he would work another hour before having lunch. As he walked across the yard toward the mower, he was the recipient of a startling message.

"Something said to me: **'You know you have lost your wallet, don't you?'** I slapped my left hip pocket. No wallet! Where could I have lost it? For the next two hours, I walked over all the area where I had cut grass. Nothing. I looked everywhere I had been, all through the house, under the beds, the couch, etc. The problem was I didn't know when I had last seen my wallet. I tried to think where I might have lost it out of my pocket. Most likely it would have been when I was sitting. I looked in the truck, under the seat and behind the seat. I went through the house again, removing the cushions from the couch. The wallet was nowhere to be found."

Nip had visited the Dillingers a few days earlier and considered the possibility his wallet might have fallen from his pocket when he got out of his truck there. His inclination was to phone them, but then decided if it had been found there, they already would have returned it. He felt most likely he had lost it while cutting grass, shredding it with the mower. He knew if this had happened, the $65 to $75 dollars in his wallet would have made nice confetti! Another thought was that Mutt had found the wallet and torn it into pieces, which now would be scattered about in his junkyard. He gave up the search, deciding he would go to Salem the next day and apply for a new driver's license and duplicate Medicare card.

"The next morning I was getting ready to head out for Salem. I was sitting on the bed and something said **'Look down.'** I just said that is about as stupid an idea as any I have ever heard. I already had looked under the bed more than once, so I went on putting on my

116

shoes. Something said again, ' **Look down!**' It was almost loud enough to hear. I said **'ALL RIGHT!'** and I looked down. There was my wallet, *on the bed rail!*"

Such experiences taught Nip that a good conversationalist doesn't do all the talking. He also must be a good listener and stay "tuned in" or he could miss hearing something very important. This applied to his conversations with Mutt and Tiger too. Nip saw Tiger coming toward him across the back yard, taking a few steps, stopping, taking a few more steps. "As Tiger got nearer, I saw he was herding a copperhead snake to me. I killed it and Tiger crawled up onto the woodpile and went to sleep. A real smart cat!"

A few days later Mutt let Nip know there was "something" in the cellar, adjoining the garage. When he opened the cellar door, Nip saw a big groundhog at the foot of the steps. "Mutt sure wanted it, but he is a smart dog and knew there wasn't enough room down there to fight. I told him that was just his problem, and I wasn't about to go down there myself. Joe Munsey (a neighbor) drove up about that time and I told him I had a groundhog in the cellar. He took a look and said it was a nice groundhog. He said he ate groundhogs and asked if I wanted to get rid of it. I said yes. He picked up a mallet (grubbing hoe), went down the steps, took one lick, and brought up the ground hog. Mutt promptly grabbed it and took off. Joe said he didn't want it anyway, but he took a few steps toward Mutt. He promptly stopped when Mutt growled and showed his teeth. I acted like I was going to head in that direction, and Mutt said if I came any closer, he would tear me limb from limb." (So much for man's best friend!)

Nip was the only person I knew who in 1995 still used a wringer washing machine. Every Monday morning he ran a hose from the kitchen sink through a window to the back porch, where he filled the washing machine and two rinse tubs. Weather permitting, he hung everything outside on lines strung across the back yard. When it rained or the temperature was below freezing, the laundry was dried inside the house. This was a time-consuming chore, but one he handled proficiently except for the morning one of his fingers got tangled up with a blanket as it was going through the wringer. He hit the control bar, releasing the pressure. Even though his finger was badly damaged, he finished the laundry before driving himself to the clinic. Eight stitches were required to close the wound, and the doctor expressed surprise that

Nip had not lost his finger. He urged him to be more careful when using the washing machine. (Good advice!)

Nip was pleased to receive a letter from AT&T with a $50 check enclosed. The letter advised that his endorsement and cashing of the check would switch his long distance phone service from his present carrier to AT&T. Since he seldom made a long distance call, it didn't matter to him which company handled them. The next day he drove to Salem and deposited the check to his bank account, smiling all the way!

Soon after depositing the AT&T check, Nip was back at the bank with another deposit. He had read in the weekly paper a dealer in gold and silver, desiring to buy old coins and jewelry, would be in Mountain Home. Nip had thirty silver dollars and a collection of coins he had accumulated while serving in Europe during WWII. He also had several pieces of jewelry of no sentimental value and a ring set with a gold nugget he had gotten during his brief stay in California. The price for gold and silver was good at that time and the "stash" brought $700. "They paid cash as they didn't want a record of how much they had on hand or something. Anyway, no receipt or anything in writing. They weighed your gold or silver, paid you in cash, and that was it. I took my seven bills to the bank and said I wanted to deposit this to my checking account. Well, first thing, they wanted to know was where I got these bills. Then they said they could only give me a temporary receipt and would mail me a deposit receipt in a day or so, which they did."

I had never seen, nor heard about, the gold nugget ring. Nip said when he was in California, he had worked about a month with the Civilian Conservation Corporation (CCC). This was similar to the WPA, but hired younger workers. Although there was a long waiting list for employment, he was able to work on a temporary basis. The job involved drilling for a tunnel through the High Sierra Mountains. For two days each week holes were drilled into the solid rock and packed with dynamite. Following the blasting, there was an entire day spent blowing in air to clear the fumes. Rubble, hauled from the tunnel in hand-pushed trolley cars, was dumped down the side of the mountain.

Every Friday employees cleared the roadways of rocks that had fallen during the blasting. There was no work on Saturday or Sunday, but there was little to do for recreation or entertainment. The nearest town was Azusa, about forty miles away, and the road was closed to all traffic. Usually the men hiked or swam in the cold water of the San Gabriel River. The area was uninhabited at that time except for a few prospectors panning for gold. Nip and some of the other young men made half-hearted attempts at panning, but it was from one of the prospectors he got the nugget for his ring. It is understandable he stayed with the CCC only one month, but what an experience for a young man!

Occasionally Nip included other "remembrances" in his letters, such as the time he cut his hand unloading milk cans at the cheese plant in Olive Branch. He went to Dr. Funderburk who cleaned the wound and instead of applying a bandage, sprayed it with something called "New Skin." Nip recalled how quickly and thoroughly his hand had healed. "While I was in his office, his daughter (probably 12 years or so old) came in. I didn't pay much attention to what was said other than the doctor said, 'Ruby Bob, tell Mother I'll be there in a little while' or something like that. Several days later I was in the store where I got paid for hauling and I was talking to a couple of boys when Ruby Bob walked in. She spoke to me, and one of the boys asked if I knew her. I said yes, that is Ruby Bob. They were both speechless, like I was a celebrity or something.

To this day I have never figured out what was so amazing about knowing Ruby Bob. She was just a little kid, probably not as old as those boys."

In the same letter, Nip continued reminiscing, "I have started rattling off about things three score or more years ago! I guess next I'll tell you about the dozen blue glass Mason jars I hid in a certain attic on my last job in Memphis. They are still there if the building is there because only I know where they are!" (Nothing further about the jars!)

Chapter 10
New Hearing Aids

January 1996 began with rain and freezing temperatures. Nip kept a fire in the kitchen stove, not only during daytime hours but also throughout the cold nights. He allowed the fire in the living room stove to burn out before bedtime as that stove did not have a grate and ashes had to be removed. However, his special "central air system," which vented heat from the kitchen stove to other rooms, kept the house comfortably warm even in the coldest weather. Additionally, heat from that stove was blown underneath the house to prevent water pipes from freezing. "Old Betsy burns 24 hours a day, sometimes it glows red hot, but it does the job."

In mid-January, Nip received word that hearing aids he had ordered some weeks earlier were ready for final fitting and pick up in Salem. Although he had worn hearing aids for many years, these were his first custom-made from molded impressions and he was eager to get them. The aids were $500 each with a two-year warranty. The molds, with a 10-year warranty, were priced at $30 each. He was pleased to receive a discount, plus three packs of batteries and cleaning supplies, for cash payment. When he had left his house that morning, the temperature was 45 degrees and the wind was gusting. After getting the hearing aids, he stopped for groceries. When he came out of the store, the temperature had dropped to well below freezing and he found a coating of ice on the windshield and doors of his truck. Sleet continued on his drive to Viola and he was thankful that he had a safe drive home.

The new hearing aids worked almost too well. He had difficulty adjusting to the many loud and strange noises he had never heard. "I started to the kitchen one morning and as I walked through the dining room something screeched like I had stepped on the cat's tail. I nearly jumped out of my skin! Of course, there isn't any cat, just a squeaking floor that I had never heard before. These odd noises all around have sort of got on my nerves at times. You just can't imagine how it is when you hear something you have never heard before, like wood cracking and popping in the stove."

Occasionally Nip wrote about his childhood days on the farm or school activities. When he was in the third grade at Capleville School he recalled his teacher, Miss Little, telling him to walk to the Clarence Bowe home, a short distance away, and bring back her green stockings. She warned him to be careful and watch for cars. Although wondering about her green stockings, he did as instructed. When Mrs. Bowe came to the door, he delivered the message. She went into her house and came back with a book. He was confused until he saw the title of the book—"Green Stockings."

He also remembered Miss Little telling him she knew he didn't have a handkerchief but to go to the boys' restroom and get some toilet paper and blow his nose real hard and quit sniffing! He did!

I had asked Nip if he remembered our paternal grandmother, Eva Pauline Little Hall. (This probably was what started his remembering Miss Little, his teacher.) He knew little more than I, but reviewed a chart our niece Sue Utley had prepared. "I then noticed Little Walter Hall died in 1921. I remember Uncle Walter, but I didn't know his first name was Little. What I remember about him is he barbecued a rabbit in the living room over the fire in the fireplace. I also remember Alice Caroline Stacy, Mammy's mother. We called her Grandmammy. I also remember Louise Fredonia Hall. She visited us when I was small. I remember Mama got mad at her for using bad language in front of us kids. She asked me to get a fresh bucket of water and Mama told her there was a full bucket of water on the separator table (where the milk separator was) and Aunt Donie, as we called her, said yes, but it was hot as p---! Mama really got her told off about that!"

Several times a week Nip's neighbors (Bridges and Dillinger families) either brought food or invited him for a meal. Charlotte Bridges kept him supplied with her homemade bread and "chicken eggs" from her mother's henhouse. She claimed store-bought eggs were all right for cooking, but "chicken eggs" were much better for eating!

Nip was surprised to find a charge of $4.45 on his telephone bill for an operator-assisted call from Cauldfield, Mo. He called the phone company to explain that he had neither made nor received a call from that location. The employee suggested possibly someone else in his household had received the collect call. "I said there is only me and my dog living here and he is an outdoor dog. I do not allow him inside the house, so he couldn't possibly have used the phone." She assured him the charge would be removed and thanked him for calling. When he received the next month's statement, he found the charge was still there. He decided

$4.45 was not worth the hassle involved in trying to get it removed from his account, so he included it with payment of his regular bill.

Mutt may not have been allowed inside the house, as Nip explained to the telephone company, but he certainly was pampered. Nip claimed Mutt would not eat dry dog food unless it was topped with cornbread or canned food, therefore every few days Nip baked a pan of cornbread. He cut it into nine pieces, six for Mutt and three for himself. As his garden began to produce, he enjoyed cornbread with fresh vegetables.

Nip was splitting wood under a big oak tree in his back yard when Mutt began barking at something in the tree. Nip assumed Mutt had spotted a squirrel but when he looked up, he saw two very big black snakes. "They were about six to seven feet long and were directly over his head. I got a pole and sort of booted them. One went back toward the tree, but the other one went toward the end of the limb. He was pretty heavy and the limb sagged a bit. Mutt leaped about six feet or more and caught that snake and yanked him down. Mutt and the snake kept striking at each other, and Mutt was getting on my nerves with all his barking. I got my garden cart and put it over the snake and pushed the part that was showing back under the cart. This got Mutt quieted, but he lay beside the cart and stayed there all evening. While he was eating his supper, I went out and looked to see if the snake was still there. It was. The next morning while Mutt was eating his breakfast, I looked again. The snake was still there so I put it into the hollow part of the tree where I seen the snakes going in earlier. I got a piece of tin and put over the hole so Mutt couldn't get to it. I think Mutt had hurt the snake, but it being a good snake (non-poisonous), I didn't want it killed. Mutt knew where it was but didn't try to dig it out. The next day Mutt started barking in the front yard. The snake was at the front steps and would strike at Mutt, about two feet each time. I tried to make Mutt leave it alone and quit barking. I finally decided the snake could just take care of itself and after a while the barking stopped. I found Mutt asleep on the porch and later saw the snake back in the hollow of the tree. I removed the tin from the hole and told Mutt to stay away and leave the snake alone. He did, however every so often he would go back and check on it. I am not fond of snakes, but I do not kill good ones."

Nip was told the Fourth of July was always celebrated with hot dogs, watermelons and fireworks in Moody, Mo., a few miles north of Viola. At the invitation of Charlotte Bridges, he found this to be true. She had said, "Wear your regular 'work clothes' and don't eat before the kids and I come by for you." Nip claimed never to have seen so many hot dogs, nor so many people. "They had three long tables—one for hot dogs, one for mustard, relish and so forth, and one for watermelons. Behind the hot dog table one lady was steadily roasting hot dogs, one was putting each dog in a small paper sack and stacking them on the table. They were already stacked the length of the table, and about a foot high. Must have been close to 1,000 already cooked and more cooking! People just helped themselves to everything. I don't know what the financial situation was. I never saw any money passed anywhere and I didn't ask." He had a great time visiting with neighbors, enjoying the music and fireworks, and eating hot dogs and watermelon.

A few days after the July 4th celebration, Nip faced a new problem. No water. He discovered this on a Sunday night when he turned on the kitchen faucet and there was not so much as a drop of water. Knowing nothing could be done about the problem until the next day, he switched off electricity to his pump and drained the water from the tank to use during the night. Additionally, "Old Betsy" had a full reservoir, so water supply was no immediate concern. He phoned Walter Dillinger for the name of the plumber he had used and assured his neighbor he had sufficient water at that time.

Early the next morning he phoned the plumber and was told he had two jobs already scheduled but would get there sometime that day. Nip asked him to bring 200 feet of plastic pipe to replace the existing steel pipe in the well. Shortly after the phone conversation, the plumber arrived. He had called his two other customers, explaining that he had an emergency to take care of before he could get to them. The hole was found about 55 feet below the pump and only three joints of the pipe were rusty. Nip then accepted the plumber's recommendation to continue with steel rather than plastic pipe, thereby having to replace only 63 feet at the bottom of the well. He assured Nip the steel pipe should last longer than the plastic and probably would be good for another 20 to 25 years. "The total cost was only $275, which was quite a bit less than it would have been with 200 feet of plastic pipe. It was all finished by 10:30 a.m. and I didn't even have to use water out of the reservoir."

On one of his visits to the Dillingers, Judy had suggested that Nip should get a microwave. Years earlier, however, when microwaves were becoming a standard kitchen fixture, Nip and Hazel had read an article that advised against microwave usage. The writer had suggested that microwaves could affect the food adversely. Nip considered Judy's suggestion when he saw a Wal-Mart advertisement listing microwaves for $88. "I thought about it some more, even decided if I ever got one, I would put it in the corner at the end of the sink, next to the dining room. There is nothing there but a stool, sort of wasted space. Then I thought about it some more and said what in the heck do I need with a microwave! I don't get in a hurry fixing a meal anyhow." (The following Christmas the Dillinger family had a big package under their tree for Nip. It was a microwave, and he soon found the convenience to be far beyond his expectation.)

I told Nip I had planned to visit Bear Creek, near Marietta, Ark. He was quick to inform me Bear Creek was near Marianna, not Marietta! He was familiar with the location because he remembered family visits with Uncle Bill and Aunt Ella Belle who lived in that area. "Aunt Ella Belle was J.O.E. Beck's only child, and their 3,000-acre plantation, Belle Meade, was named for her. Uncle Bill oversaw the plantation and ran the commissary. He gave us kids a big sack of candy from the store. They had barrels and barrels of flour in the store and all kinds of food and supplies. I think Aunt Ella Belle moved to Memphis after Uncle Bill died. I visited her a few times at 2021 Nelson. Our cousin Pauline used to go there as it was in walking distance of their home at 901 Meda Street. (Incidentally, Beck's full name was James Otis Edward Beck, and some called him Joe; others Jim.)"

Continuing his reminiscence: "I believe by the time you were born, Daddy had about quit taking all these trips. We used to all get in the back of the truck (Model T, of course, about 1922 model) and go somewhere on an all-day picnic trip. Mammy and Pa usually went also. We had quilts and always plenty of stuff to eat. One time we went to Alligator, Miss., a small town below Tunica, then west toward the Mississippi River to where Daddy said he used to go fishing in Hushpuckney Bayou. Another time we went to a branch of Coldwater River, down near Independence (called Bucksnort) and caught a lot of fish, mostly with cane poles and cork floats. We also went to Grand Junction, Tenn., to see some of Mammy's friends. Another time we went to Hansenhurst Park, which used to be where Bolton, Tenn., is now. There was a big park there, with swimming pool and slides and swings and so forth. Bolton College was there then."

It is strange how someone nearly ninety years of age can recall times, incidents, events from childhood. It proves the importance of families sharing time together, making memories to last a lifetime, however long that may be.

"Every summer after the crops were laid by, we usually went on a picnic vacation trip to somewhere. I remember one time when we went on a long trip down in Mississippi. Uncle Sam and the Joneses were going in their car, a big Dodge. Daddy was driving a Model T and leading the way. I was riding in Uncle Sam's car. He finally pulled off the road and parked in the shade under a tree. He said he wasn't going to burn up his car trying to keep up with Daddy, who he said drove like a maniac. I guess he must have been going about 25 or maybe 30 miles per hour. Uncle Sam wasn't used to driving on country roads and when he saw a car coming, he would pull over as far as he could and stop until the other car got by."

There are times when "old age" has its advantages. Nip soon found one of the busiest places in Viola was the barbershop, where usually several men waited to have their hair cut. Other customers were there to buy dog food, the sale of which was secondary business. For years after moving to Viola, Nip drove to Salem for haircuts. That was before he learned about the shop in Viola. On one of his visits there he told the barber he needed both a haircut and a 50-pound sack of dog food. While he was paying the barber, a young man, waiting to have his hair cut, walked over to Nip and asked which truck was his. He then picked up the sack and put it into the truck. At that time the barbershop did not have running water, although this later was added, and a haircut was only $2.00.

When the owner of a service station in Viola died, Walter Dillinger suggested Nip buy the station, and he would operate it for him. Nip said he didn't have enough money for such a purchase, but Walter said he had heard otherwise and questioned the rumor that Mr. Hall was rich. Nip replied, "I don't know where anyone could get that idea. I don't even own a car, don't have much of anything of value, not even a microwave. I drive a worn-out antique truck and raise most of my own food. I shop at Dollar General for anything I have to have. However, I am not hungry and I have enough clothes to stay warm, so I suppose you could say I am rich!"

All his claims were true; however, his truck had been well cared for and still had many miles to go. It was true he did not own a microwave at that time nor did he have an air-conditioner, although he failed to mention that. He was correct in saying he grew most of what he ate, for his little garden flourished. He planted and harvested a variety of vegetables for his freezer and for sharing with his neighbors. In addition to corn, peas, beans, greens and other vegetables, his cantaloupes and watermelons were plentiful, as were apples, cherries, peaches and pears. Blackberries, dewberries and raspberries took a portion of the space in his two freezers. One of the primary things he purchased at the grocery was ice cream, preferably chocolate, and he allowed himself this luxury on a daily basis—often two or three times a day. The other thing he regularly bought was bread for breakfast toast and for sandwiches. With his vegetables he preferred cornbread, which he baked both for himself and for Mutt. In many ways he was indeed a rich man, and his wonderful neighbors added much to his wealth. He enjoyed many meals with the Dillinger and Bridges families and was invited into their homes for everyday activities as well as special occasions. Additionally, at least once a week either Judy or Charlotte would appear at his door with a pot of soup, a loaf of freshly baked bread, or even an entire meal. Living in the country has many advantages!

One evening after Charlotte Bridges and her children had been visiting with Nip, he realized he was not hearing through his left ear. Thinking the battery in his hearing aid was dead, he reached to remove it and was surprised it was not in his ear. He was puzzled as to how he could have lost it. He remembered having worn his knit toboggan cap when he went outside to feed Mutt. Probably when taking off his cap, he knocked off the hearing aid. He looked unsuccessfully on the back porch where he had hung his cap. "I searched the floors in every room and then decided the next place to look would be the fix-it shop where I had been cutting kindling before feeding Mutt. It already was dark so I got my jacket and flashlight. Then I thought I had better do like Sue did with the flat tire. Better pray first, then look. I took off my jacket and prayed, then got my flashlight and looked under the couch and picked up my hearing aid. I guess Bailey knocked it out of my ear when hugging me, rubbing my head and kissing me goodbye." (Sue is our sister's daughter. Bailey is the daughter of Charlotte and Tom Bridges.)

On Thanksgiving Day, 1996, Nip was invited to have dinner with the Dillingers and afterwards went home with enough food for several meals. Along with turkey and dressing, and a variety of vegetables, his "take-out" included bread pudding with raisin sauce, pumpkin pie, pecan pie, and chocolate pie.

Soon after getting home, Nip went outside to feed Mutt. Apparently the dog was excited to see him (or maybe it was the food!) and jumped up as Nip was filling the bowl. One of Mutt's eyeteeth slashed the back of Nip's hand. Blood poured from the wound as he hurried into the house. When he realized his efforts to stop the bleeding were to no avail, he phoned the Dillingers. He explained he needed someone to take him to the emergency room in Salem. Walter had gone with Marty to deliver a load of hay, but Judy said, "I'm on the way." Within minutes she was there with a big towel that she wound tightly around his hand, telling him to apply pressure as she drove to the hospital. After the bleeding was under control and the wound cleaned, x-rays were taken to assure that no bones had been broken. Nearly a dozen stitches were required to close the wound. He left the hospital with antibiotic tablets to take that night and the next day until he could have a prescription filled for additional medication. The bandage was to be changed and ointment applied three times daily until the stitches were removed. The doctor asked if someone would be available to change the bandage. Judy would be leaving the next morning to visit relatives in Kansas City, but she told the doctor this would not be a problem. Upon reaching home, she phoned Charlotte Bridges. Within minutes Charlotte was at Nip's door with a pumpkin pie and assurance she would be there the next day to change the bandage.

That was the second time Mutt had caused Nip to make a trip to the hospital. He evidently was more than a little "put out" with the dog. He wrote, "Mutt better step lightly or I am going to kick his dog-butt." Other than this unfortunate experience, Nip had a great Thanksgiving.

Following instructions he had been given at the hospital, Nip went to his doctor's clinic eight days later to have the stitches removed. A nurse asked if the dog had been vaccinated for rabies. Since he had not, she warned if the dog had rabies, Nip should take shots within ten days of being bitten. "When I got home I was going to ask Mutt if he had rabies, but he had disappeared. After missing a couple meals, he came back and I asked him if he had rabies, and he said he had never seen a rabies."

Fortunately, Nip's hand healed well and he continued with all his usual chores. He found he could wash dishes with one hand and continued his Monday routine of washing clothes and hanging them to dry. Although Judy had a washer and dryer and offered to do his laundry, he assured her he could manage fine and he did!

As had become customary, Nip enjoyed the Christmas holidays with his neighbors. He accepted an invitation for Christmas Eve supper with the Bridges family and began Christmas Day with breakfast at the Dillingers' house, where he spent the day except for brief trips home to keep the fires going in his wood-burning stoves. Both neighbors showered him with an assortment of gifts and he, in turn, took pleasure in having presents not only for the adults, but also for the children. With sisterly help, his shopping and gift-wrapping had been accomplished early to avoid the possibility of winter weather conditions preventing travel from Memphis to rural Arkansas.

Chapter 11
The Big Fire

Nip had a sinking feeling on a windy March afternoon when he stepped into his back yard and realized what he had thought to be fast-moving clouds actually was thick smoke. Fire was racing toward the house from his woods, the flames being fanned by a brisk west wind. Hurrying in that direction, he saw Marty Dillinger attempting to battle the oncoming fire with nothing more than a garden rake. Driving home from St. Louis, Marty had seen the smoke from as far as Moody, Mo. As soon as he had reached his own house, he quickly parked his truck and ran to help his neighbor. From a distance Walter Dillinger could see the fire was out of control and he urged his son to run to safety. In the meantime, Nip had gone back to his house and phoned the Viola Fire Department. In less than 15 minutes a forest ranger arrived and asked how to get to the fire the quickest way. As the ranger was calling on a "walkie-talkie" for men and equipment, a "lowboy" with a huge bulldozer was already within sight. As the dozer operator cut trenches along the edges of the fire, some worked with rakes and others began lighting "back fires."

The ranger asked how the fire had started. Nip said he thought his neighbor (Dillinger) had been burning brush and the fire had gotten out of control. Later they saw Walter and Marty at the back of the woods, battling to keep the fire from spreading onto Van Brown's property. Nip was concerned to see blood running down one side of Walter's face. Fortunately he had not been badly injured, but scratched by a limb that narrowly missed his left eye.

When the fire in Nip's woods seemed under control, the equipment was moved to Marty's property where his woods was still burning. They had just gone through the gap that separated the properties when fire broke out again on Nip's side of the fence. Rather than waste time going back through the gap, Marty told the dozer operator to go through the fence. He said he would make repairs later. According to Nip, the dozer snapped the fence wire and ran through small trees as though they were not there. When the men felt the fire was burning itself out and there was no further danger of it spreading, they decided it was safe to leave. They came back to check on the situation a couple hours later.

The ranger asked Nip if he planned to prosecute. He said no, as he knew the fire was accidental. He was dismayed, however, when he found three ricks of wood he had cut and stacked had burned. Miraculously, wood he had stacked at the northeast corner of his property had survived the fire, although it had burned to the edge of the rick. The bark on some pieces was scorched, but none had burned.

Although the experience had left Nip physically and emotionally drained, he was thankful for those who had worked to control the fire and grateful that his house had been spared.

The fire had been traumatic, but Nip's routine soon was back to normal, i.e. wash on Monday, iron on Tuesday, have oatmeal every morning for breakfast (with one cup of instant coffee and at least two slices of toast), cut wood for the stoves and keep the fires going day and night during the cool weather.

In the early spring, after hearing Charlotte say she liked his lilac bushes and wished she had one, Nip dug several of his and transplanted them in the Bridges yard.

On one of his visits in the Bridges home, Charlotte challenged him to a game of "Marbles and Dice." This was a new game for him and he was excited to have won. (This would cause one to wonder if there was an intentional loss on her part.) During the game, a die had rolled onto the floor. "Charlotte merely picked it up with her foot (she was barefooted), just like a monkey would have done." Before leaving, he had supper with the family and was given custard pie to take home. Enjoying many meals with neighbors, it wasn't long until Nip was gaining weight and having to buy larger pants and overalls. "I guess you would say that I am getting too big for my britches."

Chapter 12
VA Pension

Although Nip had been approved in 1994 to receive a VA pension based on his physical condition, in the spring of 1997 he was informed that his case was under review and payments likely would be discontinued. According to letters received from the VA, his financial situation indicated he was not eligible for a pension. At the time of application and subsequent approval, he had been told his finances had no bearing on the matter, as the pension was based entirely on his physical condition. The letters received from the VA were quite upsetting to him, not that the pension would be discontinued but that he might be accused of false statements. "If they want their money back, I might give it back in installments like they gave it to me! No, actually I have enough in the savings account to cover it all if they want it all at once. They may be 6 months yakking about it before they decide what to do."

Nip was disturbed by a letter he had received from the V.A., signed by a Mr. Iddings.

"Mr. Iddings says it is a serious offence to misrepresent or give false information and could result in a fine or imprisonment, so maybe I'll be going to prison! I have not given any false answers at any time though. They have never asked about anything except income, and I have filled out the income papers to the cent, just like for IRS, every time they have sent me the blanks to fill out. He wrote asking the amount I have in stocks, bonds and CDs, and he decided that I have too much interest income to be in the poverty bracket!"

Although worrying about the pension situation, Nip continued his regular routine and spent many days cutting wood for his stoves with Mutt as his constant companion. One day when Mutt's barking had gotten on his nerves, he looked and found the dog was aggravating a big black snake. Every time Mutt got close, the snake would strike at him, almost getting his nose. "Mutt was quick as the snake though. I told him to leave the snake alone, but he kept barking at it. I told Mutt to shut up or I was going to tie his mouth shut. He thought maybe I meant it and came on up to where I was. Mutt doesn't like snakes and I am afraid he is going to be bitten by a copperhead some day."

One might think there would be little to write about, but Nip's weekly letters were always filled with detailed accounts of his adventures, trials with Mutt, and frequent visits with neighbors and their extended families.

From a letter of May 1997: "Judy called about 11:00 a.m. Sunday morning, Mothers Day, and asked what I was doing. I said nothing, just reading. She said well, just come over about 1:00 p.m. or 1:30 and Walter will be cooking hamburgers and hot dogs on the grill outside. I said I would be there, and she said it would probably be about 1:30 or later as they would be sort of waiting for Michael. He has a church in Missouri and wouldn't be leaving there until after 12:00 noon, and probably would go home after church. Anyhow we sure had plenty to eat—baked beans, potato salad and so forth, also pies and cakes, and someone (Judy's sister, I think) brought a dishpan full of chocolate chip cookies. Must have been about three gallons!

"Sheila (Judy's daughter) gave me a picture of that new-born son. He really is a cute little fellow. I forget what his first name is, but the middle name is Dillin, the first part of Walter and Judy's name, just left off the 'ger.'

"I stayed there for quite a while. They seem to enjoy my company. Michael came out on the patio where I was talking to Walter and Marty and said for me to go in and get started as he was getting hungry. They always want me to be first in line when we eat. I got my plate and loaded it and went into the dining room and sat down. Judy asked if I wanted tea or coffee or lemonade. I said tea would be fine. She came back with it and saw that I wasn't eating and asked if I wanted something else. I said no, that I was just waiting for the preacher to give thanks. She said Oh, and called Michael. He came in and stood at the table and gave thanks. Then he said 'I'll be right with you' and he headed back to the kitchen.

"When I left, Judy insisted that I at least take a hot dog home for supper. Of course that meant a plate lunch—beans, potato salad, slaw and so forth."

The letter continued with a report on the conversation he had with Walter and Michael. Walter had mentioned that their revival services had been well attended, and Nip had asked if there were many rolling in the aisles. Walter said no, however some were nearly overcome and some were speaking in tongues. He then asked if Nip had ever been to church services where people spoke in tongues. "I said yes, I have several times in Memphis as we had friends who were members of a Pentecostal church. I said I do not argue the tongues part; however you say they have an interpreter so the rest can understand the meaning. Well, the Bible says that everyone understood in his own language. They didn't need an interpreter. Michael spoke up and said, 'Well, that is something to give some serious thought to.'"

Memorial Day in small towns usually is celebrated as Decoration Day, a time for cleaning cemeteries, putting bright floral arrangements on the graves, and "dinner on the ground," followed by gospel singing. Viola is no exception and many former residents join the locals at Mt. Calm Cemetery every year for the big day. Nip enjoyed both the array of food and the fellowship with neighbors, even though he wasn't acquainted with some of them.

"I am amazed that so many people know me, and I don't know them! There were people on every side who would shake hands and say, 'Good to see you, Mr. Hall' or 'How are you, Mr. Hall?' Some introduced themselves. Some assumed I knew them. One little old lady said, 'So you are Mr. Hall. I have heard a lot about you. I am Mrs._____.' I don't know what she said her name is. The gossip sure gets around in these small towns."

Nip wondered if he had a visitor from outer space when the door chimes rang and he looked out to see someone in his front yard. He had headphones on both ears and wore a big backpack, from which rose a dome about twelve inches in diameter. A three-foot antenna was atop the dome. The man who had rung the door chimes looked "normal" according to Nip and he explained that he and his "alien-appearing" partner were working in the area, making note of every utility pole in Sharp, Izard and Fulton Counties. The two communicated by "walkie-talkie" and before leaving told Nip his utility pole had been installed in 1949.

Neighbor Walter Dillinger related to Nip that he had warned his son Marty, who drove an 18-wheeler, to be on the alert when in Memphis. According to him, Memphis had "more thugs and hold-up men" than any city he knew of. He said Marty had been robbed only once, and that was in Memphis. No doubt he thought Nip was wise to move away from such a terrible city.

Chapter 13
Warnings for Mutt

The weekly paper kept Nip informed not only of local activities, but also news of happenings in neighboring Missouri. He read that the postman (or woman) would not deliver mail to a house where there was a dog not chained or in a fenced yard. If there was a complaint for non-delivery, the police were notified and the owner was fined.

Nip warned Mutt. "I told Mutt he had better stay hid if they pass that law here, or rather enforce it, because maybe he is illegal anyhow. I know he is supposed to have a tag and be vaccinated, but he said if a vet tried to vaccinate him, he would come up short of an arm." (It is quite amazing how Nip and Mutt communicated!)

A few days later Mutt appeared in the yard with something in his mouth that Nip thought at first glance was a rabbit. When looking closer, he realized Mutt had killed a baby deer. "I told him off. I said 'Boy, you had better get that out of sight in a hurry. I am not a bit proud of you. You know better than to kill those deer. It is too small, out of season, and you don't have a license, not even a dog license. You could get in really big trouble if you get caught with that one, and I couldn't help you.' I don't know what he did with it, but he knew I wasn't a bit pleased, and he hid it somewhere. He sure didn't eat it because he was waiting in the garage for his supper about an hour later."

Although Nip always paid his truck insurance, it provoked him that the premium was increased every year. "That is the most useless waste of money I know of. I have never in my life derived one cent in return for the thousands of dollars paid. I have never turned in a claim. I haven't had an accident of any kind in the last half century, so what am I paying for? Oh well, I guess it is sort of like having a raincoat even if you never have to go outside when it is raining."

Nip couldn't complain about the cost of a haircut, though. The local barber in Viola charged $3.00, and he sold dog food in his shop as a side business. Nip timed him and found an average haircut took 13 minutes. Allowing another minute or two for collecting the money, this would average approximately $12 per hour or $96 for an eight-hour day. He only cut hair about five hours a day, however, except for Saturdays when he usually was open eight hours or more, and he was closed on Sundays and Mondays.

In the summer of 1997, after several letters from the Veterans Administration stating an investigation was underway concerning his eligibility to receive a pension, Nip was notified his financial status made him ineligible. Dr. Carl Arnold, his primary physician, assured Nip his pension had been approved based on his physical condition and said he would assist him in getting this matter corrected. Nip refused to allow him to intercede, even though he had been notified that he must repay all monies received or face serious penalties. Although legal assistance was offered, he refused to accept it and cashed two certificates of deposit in order to return a total of $12,526 received over an approximate 3-year period. On August 11, 1997, Nip received an official receipt from the V.A. marked "Paid in Full." An envelope was enclosed for his convenience if he wished to write, and an 800 number he could call, if he wanted to communicate. "I do not want to write. I do not want to call. I do not want to hear from them ever again."

Those were his final words at the time; however over subsequent years, he often commented about the unfair treatment he had received.

Prior to that summer Nip never had air-conditioning in his Viola home. He depended upon a ceiling fan and open windows, which he closed when the outside temperature was higher than inside the house. Marty Dillinger volunteered a window unit he no longer needed and offered to install it for Nip. At first Nip refused, but as the temperature rose to an all-time high, he relented. It didn't take long for him to realize what he and Hazel had missed all those years. The following summer he bought an air conditioner for his bedroom!

Deer roamed freely on the Hall property as no hunting was allowed. Nip's orchard produced more fruit than he could use and he was glad to share it. Sometimes, however, the deer became too possessive and seemed to forget whose fruit they enjoyed.

"I had a disagreement with a deer out back. I went to close the back door and a couple of deer were picking apples off of my best apple tree. I stepped out into the yard and yelled for them to get away from that apple tree. One old buck just pawed the ground and brayed like a horse, and acted like he was going to attack me. I said, 'If you start this way, I am going to take that garden hoe and really lay it on you; might even use the blade end of it.' The other deer left, but that one brayed a couple more times and pawed the ground. Mutt was on the front porch, so I called him. He came around the house and I said, 'Let's get him, Mutt.' and he looked at the deer and then at me. I picked up one of Mutt's old bones and threw it at the deer, and Mutt went after him. The deer decided to leave in a hurry. Mutt took it to the back fence and then came back. Some of these deer are getting too bold and I think maybe also a bit dangerous. It used to be they would run when you just went outside. Oh, well, nothing is like it used to be!"

One thing that never changed was Nip's commitment to tithing his income. Early every month, after his Social Security check had been received and all interest payments banked, he carefully figured his total income and divided one-tenth of it among 10 to 12 charities that he considered legitimate and worthy of his assistance. His favorite was N.C.O, which he referred to as "Helping Hands." Although there was an office in Ash Flat, the executive director, Mrs. Jennie Lee Stobaugh, lived in Batesville. Whenever she was in the vicinity of Viola, she called Nip and asked if she could visit. Of course he always welcomed her. On a 1997 visit, she commented to a friend who accompanied her that Nip was one of their oldest continual contributors, having never missed a month sending a donation in more than 25 years. (Note: This continued throughout his lifetime. He wrote the final check only two days before he died.)

Nip believed strongly in prayer and was an active member of the Prayer Power Club. "When several get together in prayer, miracles can really happen. When I call or write the Prayer Power Club, each member calls other members, who call still other members, and so on, and in a short while they are all praying for a specific person. Prayer works every time; however, sometimes not in the way you expect."

A late summer thunderstorm brought much welcome cooler weather, but with it came trouble for Nip. Lightening struck his well, and for the second time within two years he faced major well repair. The plumber replaced the existing plastic pipe with 198 feet of stainless steel and informed Nip that he had approximately 158 feet of water. With a bucket of drinking water and hot water in the reservoir of "Old Betsy," Nip had been fine while waiting two days for the plumber. The total bill was $855.

Although Mutt was good company for Nip, he wasn't any help in an emergency. Nip was sawing logs in the woods and stopped to pick up rocks underfoot. When he bent over to pick up the saw, the handle of the log lifter came up and struck him just above the right eye. What happened next is best told in his own words as an example of the very detailed letters he wrote. "Blood poured, but luckily I had a fairly clean rag in the trailer. I slapped it over the eye and cheek, got on the tractor, put it in 5th gear and headed for the house. I got a clean towel and put it over the wound. I called Walter; nobody home. Called Marty; nobody home. Called Tom; nobody home. So I got the door fastened and got in my pickup and headed for Salem. Let me tell you, it is something to drive a vehicle with one hand, it having a manual shift. In the meantime, the towel was becoming red, also my chin and so forth. Well, I made it fine even though I got behind one slow poke. I didn't wait for a passing lane, I just pulled over the center line and went by. He looked at me and I guess saw all the blood and nearly ran off the side of the highway. It was sort of hard to see correctly with one eye. Well, I saw the clinic was loaded, so I never slowed down, just went to the ambulance entrance of the hospital. There was a paramedic putting supplies in one of the ambulances. After I parked, I went to where he was and asked if I was considered an emergency. He looked at me and took me by the arm and said that it sure looked that way. We went into the emergency room and he said for me to sit there on the cot. Then he said for me to take the compress off. I did, and the blood started to flow, so he said to put it back, and he handed me a hospital towel. In the meantime, the nurse had got her clipboard and started the usual round of questions—name, address, phone number, etc. I got out my wallet and took out my Medicare card and list of medicine I was taking and handed them to the paramedic. He nodded and put them in the copy machine and made copies and handed them back and gave the copies to the nurse. She was still asking stupid questions like 'What is your Social Security number?' etc. I just said, 'Look at the card in your hand.' She said 'Oh,' and asked who was my nearest kin. I said 'Anne H. Norris, sister. Address: 8120 North Pole Cove, Memphis, TN 38125. Phone number: (901) 753-5737 and my doctor is Carl Arnold, address: Salem Clinic, next door.' She looked at me for a minute and the phone rang. She answered it and said for me to report to Dr. Carl Arnold at his office immediately and asked if I could get there by myself. I said yes and left. I drove next door and walked in. The nurse there asked if I could sign in. I said yes, and signed in.

"We went directly to one of the examining rooms and in a few minutes Dr. Arnold came in and asked what had happened. I told him. He asked if I had been wearing glasses. I said yes. He asked if they broke and cut my face or eye. I said I did not know. He asked where my glasses were. I said I have no idea. They are somewhere in the woods where I was working, probably broken. He removed the compress I had on and said close your eyes, and he started saturating my face with something. Then said, well it looks like nothing much, mostly a scratch and bruise, and then he put some triple anti-biotic ointment on my face and wrote a prescription for antibiotic to be applied three times a day. I had plenty of that at home, so I didn't stop at the drug store, just headed for home. The receptionist was talking on the phone, so I didn't even stop, just put my file on the desk, waved at her and left. I *thought* that was fairly quickly over with. Well, by the time I got home, the blood was running into my eye and dripping off of my chin. I got inside, grabbed a clean rag (an undershirt), held it over my eye and drove back to the clinic. Dr. Arnold asked what happened. I said I didn't know; it just started bleeding, apparently from above my eye as it was running into my eye. He went through the same procedure again and said there was a cut above my eye, between the eyelid and eyebrow, probably from broken glasses. He got that fixed and said he was off the rest of the day, but Griffin Arnold would be there if needed. Carl only works till noon, and it was a bit past 12:00. He told me to just sit where I was for one hour before I left again. A few minutes after he left, Griffin came in and asked what the trouble was. I told him Dr. Carl had said for me to just sit where I was for one hour. He asked what had happened. I told him. He said he had used a log lifter, but never had one kick back. I said I have used this one for over 25 years and couldn't explain how it had happened unless maybe the log had rolled slightly.

"Well, about an hour later, the nurse came in and said OK, you can go. I said Thank You and left again. As I passed the receptionist she was on the phone again, but sort of indicated I should wait a minute. I just shook my head, twinkled my fingers at her and kept going. When I got home, it was too late for dinner. Besides I had just about lost my appetite, so I just got a mug of ice cream from the freezer, then went out and got on my tractor and headed for the woods to see if I could find the remains of my glasses. When I got there, I sat on the tractor and prayed for God to show me where the glasses were. I got off and went to where I had been standing. I carefully raked all the leaves from the spot for about 10' x 10'. No glasses, so I said that regardless of what shape they were in, I needed the glasses. Then I stepped over the log and saw the glasses, about eight or ten feet from the log. Intact. Not a scratch on them!

"Well, since all my tools were still in the cart, I said this log isn't going to bug me. I got out my chain saw and cut the entire log up, without using the log lifter. Then I went home and put everything away and fed Mutt and thought I would call it a day. I almost did, but something else came up. I started to apply the ointment, and I took off my glasses, and then I couldn't tell where I was putting the ointment. I tried applying the ointment with the glasses on, but about all I was doing was smearing up the glasses, so I went to the phone and called Judy. She and Marty came and she put the ointment on and Marty cleaned my glasses. Judy asked how I would manage the next day. I said I would figure that out. The next morning I thought about that magnifying mirror in the bathroom. With it I could see where I was putting the ointment so no problem.

"Well, everything is fine now. There is a sore place on the side of my nose where the glasses hit it. I am very fortunate and thankful."

Details of such experiences and everyday events were reported in Nip's letters that fill the shoeboxes on the closet shelf.

Chapter 14
Nip's Good Humor

Nip celebrated the Christmas holidays with both the Bridges and Dillinger families and began the year 1998 in good spirits and good health. Perhaps his humor contributed to his condition, both physical and mental.

"I got a card from the American Hosiery Company, or rather a double card, addressed to Mrs. Frank P. Hall. It said, 'We haven't a clue as to why you haven't sent in the other card we sent you for your free Silkie panty hose. They are absolutely free, no charge, nothing to buy, etc. etc.' Signed by Eve Stoneburg. Well, just for the heck of it, I mailed the card back with a note. 'Dear Mrs. Stoneburg. This card you sent says you folks haven't a clue, etc. Please let me clue you in on this matter. Mrs. Frank P. Hall died October 13, 1993, so doesn't need panty hose. I am sure she would like Silkies, but she is now resting in Mount Calm Cemetery. I hope this will clear your mind on this matter. I appreciate your thoughtfulness. Sincerely, Mr. Frank P. Hall.'"

Nip found if his phone rang only three times and he did not answer, usually the party would hang up. He figured the call most likely would be from a charitable organization and the caller would not want to leave a message on a recorder. Sometimes he would answer anyway and pretend he misunderstood the message. He would tell the caller he was an old man, living on a small pension, and any help they could send would be appreciated.

"One day after four rings I answered the phone and the caller (a lady) asked if this was the residence of Mr. Frank P. Hall. I told her it was indeed his residence. She asked if Mr. Hall was at home. I replied, 'Yes, he sure is.' Then she asked if she might speak with him. I said 'Certainly. In fact you are speaking to him at this time. I am Frank P. Hall and this is my residence.' I felt certain she was trying to sell something, but decided to see what she had to say. She explained she worked for a home improvement company and they would like to put vinyl siding on my house. I said I wasn't interested in siding. She then suggested I might need new windows. I said, 'Lady, this shack I am living in was built before World War II, out of unfinished sawmill lumber, and it isn't worth one new window. I am 84 years old and couldn't possibly enjoy many years if my house had new windows.' She apologized for calling, but I assured her it was all right. In fact, I thanked her for calling and wished her a nice day and good luck with her sales. Before I could hang up the phone, she thanked me and said I was the first person she had called who wasn't absolutely rude if not interested in siding or windows."

While many people will not open their door when they see two people (usually young men) carrying Bibles and/or other material, this never was the case with Nip. He not only opened the door, he invited them into his house. He delighted in discussing religion. When one such visitor admired Nip's Bible with four versions of Scripture, saying he hoped to someday be able to afford such, Nip gave it to him. He lived his faith every day, never doubting God was in control.

One day a small white pickup truck, unfamiliar to Nip, stopped in front of his house. The driver, whom Nip thought was a lady because of the long blond hair and delicate features, remained in the truck. Presuming "she" was afraid of Mutt, Nip went outside to see who had come calling. He was surprised to see the beautiful curly, shoulder-length hair belonged to a young man. He stepped out of the truck when Nip assured him Mutt would not bite. He said the owner of the property across the road from Nip had given permission to dig sumac bushes. Nip considered the man must be a bit nutty until he explained that he made walking sticks and the sumac roots, running parallel to the ground, were excellent for that purpose. He showed Nip a few of the walking sticks he had made and said he had sold hundreds of them. The man dug sumac roots until it became too dark to work, then returned the next several days for more. On his final trip, he gave Nip a beautiful sumac walking stick. Nip may never have used it, but he appreciated the gift. (Note: After Nip's death, the sumac walking stick became the possession of nephew Adam Hall.)

Nip was mystified when Mutt appeared in the yard with a plastic grocery bag, carrying it upright so as not to spill the contents. "When I started that way to see what he had, he indicated he would chew me up if I got too close. Mutt finally took a bone from the bag and headed toward the barn. While he was out of sight, I went down to see what he had. It was a batch of fresh bones that had all the meat removed, like from a butcher shop." Nip didn't disturb Mutt's treasure, and Mutt seemed to enjoy the bones for several days.

Several days later Nip saw a well-filled Wal-Mart grocery bag on the road bank, near his mailbox. "When I walked over that way, Mutt said it would be very unwise for me to get too close to his property. He proceeded to rip a hole in the bag and he pulled out what looked like a big uncooked biscuit. He almost choked on it, but got it down and pulled out another one. About half an hour later I saw he was gone, so I quietly went out to take a look. That bag was completely full of large raw biscuits."

Nip could not imagine where Mutt had gotten the biscuits and he feared he would choke on them. He knew Mutt liked cooked biscuits so decided to cook them for him. He oiled some baking pans and fired up Old Betsy. The biscuits were big and smelled good, but he was afraid to eat them himself. There were 72 biscuits, nearly filling a five-gallon can when cooked.

He asked the Dillingers if they knew anything about the biscuits. They did not, and the mystery continued until he learned from Tom Bridges that while he and Charlotte were out of town, their freezer had thawed, having somehow been unplugged. Tom had tossed the bag of biscuits beside the road, thinking Mutt would take care of them, and he did. Nip rationed them to Mutt, giving him one each morning with his breakfast and another with his supper until the supply was depleted. Nip figured the bones also had come from the Bridges freezer. Big mystery solved!

No one ever had a bigger heart than Nip and he always was willing to help those less fortunate. "There was an old lady at the grocery when I was in line to pay. She had a few items in her cart and instead of putting them on the counter, she handed the checker all her food stamps and dumped all the change out of her little change purse onto the counter. She asked the checker if she had enough to get a pound of pinto beans. The checker looked in her cart and counted her change and food stamps and said yes, so she pushed the cart aside and said 'Excuse me' to me and went back to get the pound of beans. I just thought about paying for whatever she lacked of having enough, but the checker must have sort of read my mind because she just sort of shook her head and said there are several just like that right here in Salem. They just barely have enough to exist. Something like this makes you really see how near starving so many people are, and how very fortunate we are. There doesn't seem to be what used to be called middle class, unless it's like me. They are either so poor they don't have enough food and clothing or they are what I call well off (and don't know it)."

Nip lamented to Walter Dillinger that he had lost one of his hearing aids, which had cost about $500. He had searched everywhere in the house, as well as outside, and decided it was hopeless to continue looking. "Before going to bed, I prayed and asked God to tell me where my lost hearing aid was. Then I went to sleep. I woke up about 12:30 a.m. and something sort of said to me to go to the kitchen and get a drink and then come back into the living room and get that 'lost' hearing aid because it needed to be turned off as it was steadily squealing. I got up in a hurry, went to the kitchen, and on out to the back porch to the refrigerator and got a drink of Kool Aid. Then I went back through the dining room, and I said I see that hearing aid over there under the rocking chair with the blue cushion. I went over there and sure enough, I did see it! I reached under the chair and picked it up and turned it off. I guess it was squealing, but of course, I couldn't hear it. I have no idea how it got there, as I don't sit in that chair. I always sit on the couch."

Nip received many requests from "charitable" organizations. He chose to give regularly to quite a few that he felt were worthy of his contributions. After having received decals from the National Law Enforcement Memorial Fund, with a suggestion he put them on his car, he had a phone call to see if he would like to send a small donation. He informed the caller that he had indeed received the decals, but had thrown them away as he had no use for them whatsoever. "I do not own a car, haven't owned a car in 28 years. I am 84 years old and haven't worked at a salaried job since 1970 so would appreciate it if you would take my name off your mailing list and I do not wish to give a small donation." Nip didn't hear the phone disconnect, but thought the caller had hung up while he was still talking because he heard "Please hang up and try your call again, etc." (It was true he did not own a car, but he had a pickup truck!)

A few days later he received a call from Captain Camerello, Commanding Officer of the Salvation Army in Mountain Home. Capt. Camerello told Nip he was aware that he recently had sent a generous donation, but said they were in an extremely serious shortage of food and supplies for the needy and would appreciate it if he could help them again. He further said if they did not immediately restock the food pantry, they would have to say no to a lot of hungry people. (Nip said his "generous donation" was $15.) "When he ran out of breath, he waited a few seconds and said, 'Mr. Hall, are you there?' I said yes, I am here, and I listened to you all the way. I am glad to help out when I can, but no matter how much of an emergency or whatever, Social Security does not get my check out until the 3rd of each month. I probably will be able to send you another donation sometime after the 3rd of next month. Best wishes and keep up the good work, Captain."

Nip's tender heart was touched by some of the pitiful tales he heard, but he often would not listen to the entire plea, interrupting to give his own spiel. That usually got rid of the solicitor.

The weekly paper (No daily newspaper in Viola!) ran a notice from the county health department, warning that it was illegal to let dogs run loose and they must have current licenses and be vaccinated for rabies. A schedule was given as to when a county veterinarian would be in each town. According to Nip, "Mutt refused to go. He said he had already been shot and could show his scar!" The scar resulted from the earlier time when he had nearly died after being shot. Mutt had never been a gentle dog, having twice sent Nip to the doctor with accidental wounds. It was in a fight and not an accident, however, that he had killed one of Marty Dillinger's beagles. Nip had told Marty at that time to shoot Mutt, but Marty said he could never do that, knowing how much Nip cared for the dog.

Chapter 15
A Love for Books

Anyone who stepped into the Hall living room would immediately surmise that someone enjoyed reading. Bookshelves lined most of the walls, floor to ceiling. Nip built narrow bookcases for the many paperback books and converted old television cabinets for books too large for the wall shelves. Shortly after he and Hazel moved to Viola, they joined a mail order book club. They soon had sets of reference books, novels, biographies, mysteries, and volumes that dealt with health and nutrition. Perhaps the most notable, however, were the many religious books and various versions of the Bible. Nip enjoyed reading the Bible and participated in a Bible course by mail. He was proud of the certificate he received when he completed the study. Often he would find something in the Bible that he had missed in previous readings and would share this with Brother Michael, the Dillingers' "preacher son," or he would include it in one of his letters, i.e. the following excerpt:

"I was reading in Genesis in the Bible about the flood, and I just happened to think that Noah might have been tempted to take on some of those innocent children and babies who were drowning, but he sure didn't have a chance to do that. After he got all those animals in, two by two, he didn't close the door. God closed the door, and when God closes a door, it is really closed. I looked it up in several versions of the Bible, and they all say that God closed the door of the Ark when the last of the animals were inside. I am forever seeing some little things that I have read a dozen times and never gave any thought to it. Then all at once I see it in a different light. The Bible becomes more interesting when you take the time to really check out small items that you have read over and over."

Nip did not often go to church services, although occasionally he went with one of his neighbors. He said it was embarrassing because he couldn't hear and didn't know what was being said. He didn't want to turn up the volume on his hearing aids for fear they would squeal and be disturbing to others.

One evening just after 7:30, Marty Dillinger stopped at Nip's house to tell him they would be having church service at 8:00 p.m. and wanted him to attend. Nip said he would like to go, but there wasn't time to get cleaned up on such short notice. No need to change clothes, Marty had told him, because the service would be at his parents' house. There would be only family there, including Brother Michael, his wife and children. They would have supper, to which Nip was invited, and then the service. Nip changed his clothes, nevertheless, and arrived at the Dillingers' as they were finishing their meal. At Marty's insistence, he had dessert—a big bowl of banana pudding.

When everyone was seated in the living room, Brother Michael got his notes and informed his congregation that the evening's subject would be "Love." Nip was favorably impressed with the young preacher's sermon. "Michael gave us a real good sermon, about an hour long, practically all about God's love for all of us. He used the 23rd Psalm for reference, and closed the service with prayer."

Marty had insisted Nip bring his book, "Lost Books of the Bible." Nip kept it out of sight until after the service. He then reluctantly showed it to Michael, but told him he did not want to influence his thinking in any way and assured him it was not his idea to bring the book to the service. After scanning the book, Michael said many people would not agree with the author, but he thought it to be of interest as were most religious books, no matter what a person's faith might be, as long as one keeps an open mind. (Note: Nip enjoyed many conversations with Brother Michael and as he had requested, at his death all his Bibles and religious books were given to this young preacher.)

Chapter 16
Trouble for Mutt

Early one morning Nip went outside to give Mutt his breakfast and the dog was not waiting at his usual place on the front porch. After calling him several times, Nip was concerned and went to the garage to see if Mutt was still in his bed. To his alarm, his canine friend was lying still with his eyes closed. Nip's first thought: Mutt's dead!

Hurrying into the house, Nip got a flashlight and returned to take a closer look. To his relief, Mutt was alive, but wouldn't open his eyes. On further examination, Nip saw Mutt's eyes had been bleeding. He lifted one lid and found the eye had a whitish glaze. He checked the other eye and found it was similar. He felt certain Mutt was blind. He helped Mutt to his feet, led him to his food pan and put it under his nose. Mutt took a few nibbles and turned his head, apparently wanting to go back to his bed.

"One of Mutt's eyes was swollen and oozing, and the other one seemed to be sealed shut. I didn't know what to do for him, so I phoned Marty. No answer, but I put a message on his recorder that Mutt was blind."

In a short while Marty rode up on his four-wheeler. Nip had to do some coaxing to get Mutt out of the garage. He would take a few steps and then stop, walking only when Nip's hand was on his head or back. When Nip got Mutt outside in the daylight, Marty took one look and said, "Fescue!"

Marty said when dogs run through a field of fescue at that time of the year, the seeds may get into their eyes. While he possibly could remove the seeds from Mutt's eyes, it would be painful and Mutt likely would bite him. He suggested Nip try splashing water on Mutt's eyes as that should help, and he probably wouldn't bite Nip.

"I got some water and managed to get some in his eyes. He seemed to know I was trying to help and stood real still. Finally he got one eye to stay open most of the time, and he came out into the yard and followed me every stop I took. I had to stop and pet him often and he would turn that closed eye toward me as if he was asking me to do something. I pulled that eye open several times and it looked all right, just sort of clouded over. I just kept telling him it was doing fine."

Nip continued to worry about Mutt's eyes, which two weeks later did not seem to have improved. "Poor old Mutt. I guess he is a one-eyed dog from now on. One eye got all right, but I believe he is about blind in the other eye. It is clouded over and still oozing a bit. He can't see very well. I have noticed he has trouble recognizing things. Yesterday he was trotting along in front of me, down toward the old ex-pond, when suddenly he stopped and sort of backed up. I looked down in front of him, and there was a stick a couple feet long on the ground. I told him it was just a stick and I picked it up and tossed it aside. He thought it was a snake. He is still active though, but requires a lot of petting since his injury." Nip later wrote that Mutt was doing fine and could see out of that eye, although not well.

One thing that may have helped with Mutt's recovery was the company he began keeping with Muffin, a small, shaggy dog that belonged to the Bridges family. Muffin began trotting down the road for daily visits with Mutt and soon was spending more time there than at his own house. It took quite a while before Mutt was willing to share his food, but the two dogs romped together, with Muffin often taking a tumble from the bigger dog. It didn't take long, however, for Nip to accept the fact he had another mouth to feed. He and Muffin became close friends.

Perhaps it was the eyesight problem that affected Mutt's disposition. He seemed to become more vicious, even snarling at Muffin on occasion. When Nip learned Mutt had been in another fight with Marty's beagles, having killed again, he knew what must be done. It was something he could not do himself, so he phoned Marty and asked for a favor. "I'll be glad to do anything I can," Marty replied. Nip said, "I want you to shoot Mutt." Marty's protests did not change Nip's mind. He knew the next time Mutt killed it could be a child, a neighbor, or even himself.

Marty found Mutt in the clearing behind Nip's house and killed him with a single shot. Muffin seemed to share Nip's sorrow, and for many days they grieved together. Muffin filled an empty spot and remained Nip's close companion throughout the coming years.

Close contact with his neighbors helped Nip as he dealt with the loss of Mutt. However, soon after Mutt's death, he had another concern. "I am sad today. My friends on top of the hill are very ill. The only one not sick is Brittany. They got her out before she caught whatever they have. Charlotte, Tom and Bailey have been sick for a week now. The doctor doesn't know what it is." (Apparently they had a virus of some kind and although Nip offered to take food, or anything they might need, his offers were refused. They did not want to expose him to whatever they all had, but he continued to want to do something for them.)

"I happened to think that maybe if I cooked a peach cobbler, some of the sick folks might eat a few bites. I cooked one on the electric stove. (I had let the fire go down in old Betsy.) When I put it in the oven, I set the timer for 45 minutes. When the time was up, I had a tray ready with a couple of 'Reminisce' magazines and a folded towel on it, and also a box of hot chocolate mix, and I took the cobbler pie up there."

Charlotte's mother met him at the door. He waved to Charlotte and Bailey, but did not go into the house. He later learned not only was Charlotte ill with whatever others in her family had, but also she was pregnant and had to be hospitalized for two days. She later told Nip others had said to let them know if they could help, but he had come to their aid without being asked, and they loved him for being such a wonderful neighbor.

"Speaking of good neighbors, nobody has better neighbors than 'Mr. Hall.' This morning for breakfast I had sausage from the

Dillingers, biscuits from Charlotte, eggs from her Mom, and finished off with a bit of molasses from Charlotte. Then after I got the dishes washed and kitchen cleaned, I had a banana from Brittany."

Chapter 17
Goodbye to Old Betsy

Nip lost another old friend that spring with the "death" of Old Betsy, the wood-burning kitchen stove that "came with the house." Not only had hundreds of Hazel's pies and cakes been baked in the oven, but also Nip's cobblers. One of the best features of Old Betsy was the reservoir. With a good fire in the stove, there would be hot water in the reservoir. Before going outside to mow grass, cut wood, or handle other chores, Nip often would select food from his freezer and drop it into the reservoir. When he went inside for lunch, the food would have thawed and usually be warm enough to eat without further heating.

He hated to see Old Betsy go, but she was beyond repair with the firebox badly cracked. Nip concluded the time had come to replace the wood-burning stove with a propane heater and use his electric range for cooking.

After checking with the Dillingers, who used propane, and talking with one of the propane dealers, Nip ordered a large heater and arranged for the rental and installation of a

250-gallon tank. Although Old Betsy was an antique, there was no way to get the stove out of the house within dismantling it. This was accomplished with the help of neighbors and a few days later all the parts were hauled away by Marty. It was another sad day for Nip, who was heard to say, "Old Betsy is no more—just a memory."

The propane heater and tank were delivered promptly. The employee set and leveled the tank and dug a trench from the tank to the house. He explained to Nip that he could not crawl underneath the house to make the connection to the stove because he was too fat. Since Marty had offered to do it, he said he would have to leave that to him. To his surprise, Nip said he could show him how to easily run the tubing without anyone going underneath the house. "I said I have a high limb pruner that has a number of four-inch extensions. It can be extended 24 inches, which is about double as long as will be needed. You can just push that tubing down through the hole in the floor. I will hold the light under the house so you can work with both hands. You just hook the pruner onto the end of the tubing and then I will go inside and feed the tubing down through the hole while you pull it out as far as you want it. When you get enough, just knock on the wall and that's it. Well, it worked, and only took about 10 to 15 minutes. He cut the tubing off at the crawl hole, got a larger size to run from the tank, joined them together, and that was it." When Marty later came to make the connection, Nip told him the work had been done!

Although the new propane heater lessened the need for stove wood, Nip continued to cut wood and always kept a supply for the small living room heater. Not only did the heater save on propane, but Nip also enjoyed cutting wood and keeping his sheds stocked with at least a year's supply at all times. He just could not give in entirely to the convenience of propane.

The air conditioning was a different matter. When the older unit, which Marty had installed for him, quit and he was not able to repair it, Nip didn't waste time before driving to Salem and buying another one. He didn't wait for it to be delivered, but had it loaded onto his pick-up truck. "On the way home, I saw Walter was home so I stopped and said I needed a bit of help for about 30 minutes. He said fine, and I told him that I had a new air-conditioner and needed some help lifting the big one out of the window. I said I could handle the rest of the job. Well, he and I took the old one out, and he said let's just put the new one in while we are at it, so we did, and got it turned on." Since Nip was going to junk the old one, Walter took it with him, saying he might work on it later. Nip feared that would not set well with Judy, who already was complaining about the clutter of junked mowers, tillers and other equipment. Walter assured him he would get the air conditioner out of sight in one of the sheds before Judy got home from work.

Less than a month later Nip again was asking help from the Dillingers. He sought Walter's opinion as to what was causing the engine of his pickup to run so noisily. As he suspected, Walter said it was the water pump. Rather than driving to Salem, he suggested Marty could buy a new water pump for him in Mountain Home. Salem's only auto supply store probably would not have one for a 1970 truck, and there were four stores in Mountain Home where Marty could stop. Although Nip said he would not need the truck for at least a week, he was surprised the next day when Marty and Walter appeared with the new pump, ready to install it. Before Nip could get a bucket into which to drain the radiator, Marty already was working underneath the truck, and Walter was busy on topside. The new water pump, which cost only $27.95, was installed in record time. Nip tried to give Marty $60, but he refused to accept any money for labor. Wanting to do something to show his appreciation, Nip later filled a big cookie jar with hard peppermints and took it to Walter, who was trying to quit smoking. Nip told him to pop a peppermint into his mouth when he had an urge for a cigarette, which he said helped him break his own smoking habit.

Nip never hesitated to call upon his good neighbors any time he needed their assistance, but he was always aware his help actually came from a Higher Source. Often he shared experiences that gave credence to this belief. Following is an excerpt from one of his letters.

"Yesterday when I was coming in from the woods on the tractor, I wasn't as careful as I should have been and lost my glasses. I was going pretty fast, in fifth gear I believe it was, and I went under a limb that struck me in my face. I stopped about 50 feet farther when I realized I had lost my glasses. I got off and went back and carefully searched everywhere in the vicinity of where the limb had smacked me but found no glasses. I then thought that maybe I had lost them back where I had last used the chain saw because I was sweating and maybe they fell off. I can see off in a distance, sort of, if I am not wearing glasses. Anyhow, I decided to go on in and get my other glasses and come back and look again. I went on in and got my other glasses. Then I thought that the thing I should have done in the first place was to ask the One who knew where the glasses were to tell me. So I prayed and said, ' Now, Lord, I need those glasses so I am asking you to show me where they are, just as you did before when I got injured and lost them.' Then I got on the tractor and went back, knowing I would find the glasses. I saw the glasses over in the weeds beside the driveway even before I got off of the tractor to look for them."

Chapter 18
Life in the Slow Lane

The days and weeks, months and years, in Nip's life continued on a somewhat routine basis. His neighbors kept the routine from being boring as he spent many hours visiting and enjoying meals with them. There were countless times when he "just happened to stop by" the Dillingers' house in late afternoon and would be invited to stay for supper. Other times he was invited to eat with the Bridges family. It is doubtful he ever turned down an invitation. He also enjoyed the companionship of Muffin, the Bridges' dog that spent more time with Nip than with her owners. Keeping an ample supply of food for Muffin provided Nip with an excuse for a trip to Salem. This too provided a diversion.

"I had to go to Salem after I got the clothes washed and hung all over the house and back porch. I didn't need a thing for myself, but was almost completely out of dog food. I have to stay with Muffin until she eats all she wants, then bring what is left inside. I failed to do that one day last week and Walter's big dog took Muffin's food and she didn't get a bite. I saw him and tried to run him away, but he wouldn't let me get close while he gobbled up Muffin's breakfast. Then he took her bowl in his mouth and headed for the road with it. This was a bit too much for me, so I got a broom and took out after him. He dropped the bowl and took off. I came back and got Muffin another breakfast and stood guard there on the front porch until she ate all she wanted. It was a good thing I did, too, because that dog had come back and poked his head around the corner of the house. I went after him again with the broom and that time he left for good. I guess he was hungry, but I am only feeding one dog."

Nip always topped off Muffin's dog food with a small amount of chicken. He regularly bought large packages of chicken thighs and legs and cooked them for Muffin. He claimed Muffin would not eat regular dog food unless he put chicken or broth on top of it. Occasionally Nip baked a can of biscuits and shared them with Muffin.

In addition to buying food for Muffin when he went to Salem, Nip usually bought four or more loaves of bread for himself. He kept several "spares" in the freezer. When it was on sale, he would buy even more—always the cheapest plain white bread. He ate a *lot* of bread! He regularly toasted three slices for breakfast, to eat with his oatmeal, would have at least two slices with his lunch, and a couple more with supper.

Although Hazel had convinced him that microwaves were dangerous to one's well being, Nip admitted he had looked at some in Mountain Home. He also had observed how handy microwaves were for his neighbors; still he resisted the temptation of purchasing one for his own use. The Dillingers took the situation in their own hands. Walter and Judy, and their extended family, gave Nip a microwave for Christmas. That was in 1999, and he soon was using it on a daily basis. He kept a supply of microwave meals in his freezer, referring to them as "TV dinners."

Nip tried dozens of different hearing aids. (He often declared to have been deaf since birth; however one might wonder how he passed the physical exam for service in WWII.) As with others who have hearing deficiency, it seemed to be tones of voice that were the primary problem. There also were certain letters that he did not hear correctly as was found when he was examined for the military pension. He found some hearing aids did not fit comfortably or did not work well. Rather than having them repaired, he usually bought new ones, having found that less expensive. Being the thrifty man he was, he never purchased the more expensive kind, claiming they all worked equally well—or not so well! He accumulated an assortment of broken or "worn out" hearing aids and also lost a few over the years.

"I was cutting broken limbs off of the plum bushes down on the 'north 40' and lost one of my hearing aids. I searched for it half a day, but I don't guess there is a possible chance of ever finding it. Sort of like looking for a needle in a haystack. Only God knows where it is. I have asked Him to show me where it is, but I haven't gotten an answer. I am thankful for having *one* hearing aid."

About three months later Nip declared he was the recipient of two real, visible miracles in the same day. "Last Sunday evening I couldn't get outside very much as it was drizzling rain. I was looking down toward the plum thicket and could see red and yellow plums. Once the rain let up, I decided to see if there were enough to pick. The ground was soggy and I was bogging down almost every step. When I got there I saw I wouldn't get more than maybe a pint. The animals had been feasting, had broken limbs and had gotten just about all the red plums and most of the yellow ones. I picked a few of the yellow ones and popped them into my mouth. I had gone around the yellow thicket and started to leave. I saw a big super-size one and picked it. Being clumsy, I dropped it and as I reached down to pick it up, I saw the hearing aid I had lost last March! It was mired down in the mud and water, so I knew it was shot. But I said now that is a *miracle*. I had cut the grass there and had run over it three times that I recall. Well, I took it to the house. The battery had rusted in it, and it was full of mud. I decided I could at least salvage the ear mould. I finally got the battery out and got some Q-tips and started cleaning it up as best I could. Then I put it on the chest in the bedroom and turned the little fan on it, with the battery compartment and everything open (that I could get opened) and forgot about it. About three or four hours later, I happened to think about it. I went in and got it and put a new battery in it. I said, 'Now, Lord, I can't say I need this hearing aid because I now have three working aids, but a second miracle would be nice.' I then put it into my ear, set it on two, where I normally wear my aids, and flipped the switch on. No, it didn't work! Oh, well, I guess you just can't have everything you want. I cleaned a few more spots of rust off and just sort of fiddled around, then tried it again. When I put it on this time, I heard a faint humming, sort of like a dying bee. I turned the volume all the way to the peg. It seemed to hum a bit louder, but that was all, so I just put it in one of the carrying cases and put it in my pocket. Well, that night I was watching 'Touched by an Angel,' and when a commercial came on, I happened to think about the hearing aid in my pocket. I got it out, set the volume on two, and put it on. When I flipped on the switch, it came on loud and clear. I think it is working better than when it was brand new! Miracle Number 2!"

In the year 2000, Nip's address changed from a rural route and box number to 460 Brentwood Lane to comply with 911 regulations. Attempting to notify the Social Security Administration was totally frustrating to him. He complained that he was only able to talk to a machine that instructed him to press a series of buttons for various options. When he finally was instructed to give an address change, he was allowed only 30 seconds and he couldn't explain his change in such a limited time. He gave up and wrote a letter. He encountered similar problems at the banks and other businesses, having to assure them he had not moved.

Other than relatives and neighbors, not too many people traveled Brentwood Lane. Occasionally someone from one of the churches knocked at his door, and he always welcomed them. "I had company today—Jehovah's Witnesses. One of them was here recently, but she had a new one along with her this time. She said she had told them about me and the discussion we had and said they had asked her to invite me to their memorial meeting and perhaps I would lead a sort of group discussion. She said she had thought about something I had said when they were here before and decided there was much truth in it, rather than criticism. I said I didn't recall anything special I had said, and she said she was referring to what I said about going to other churches like Catholic, Presbyterian, Baptist, and so forth and that some people would not want to learn any more about the Bible or religion because they were convinced that they were 100% right and all others were wrong. I said 'Oh, yes, I remember that. I believe you or the other lady asked which church I attended, and I said a couple weeks ago I went to the Mitchell Church of Christ, but I also have attended Baptist, Methodist, Catholic, Jewish and others as you can learn something from every one of them if you have an open mind.' The lady gave me a card with date, time and location of Kingdom Hall in Salem and told me that everything was free— that they didn't take up a collection like some churches do. I didn't say anything. Of course I have no intention of going, but no reason for any more yak about it."

On a visit with Walter and Marty, Nip mentioned that he had no problem cutting grass with his riding mower, but with so many trees and bushes, trimming was a big job. Marty said, "Mr. Hall, you call me when you start trimming and I will be there with my weed-eater. The two of us can get it done a lot quicker." Nip told him he appreciated the offer but there was no rush to do the work. He added, "However, when I get old, I just might take you up on it." He never did. When he later saw Walter's yard needed trimming attention, he took his weed-eater and trimmed for his neighbor.

On one of his late afternoon visits with the Dillingers, he was asked (as always!) to stay for supper. (He did.) He later explained, "Judy had a lot of real thin sort of dough disks, about 12 inches in diameter, and she shaped them like bowls and baked them. They were almost as thin as potato chips. She motioned for me to come into the kitchen. She had one of those baked bowls and started filling it with tomatoes, lettuce, some kind of dressing, etc. The food was really good, mostly fresh vegetables and the bowl also was edible!"

Always ready with a helping hand for the less fortunate, be it man or beast, Nip reported an unusual experience. "Yesterday I did a job that I never heard of anyone doing. I repaired a turtle's shell, or rather, a terrapin's shell. I saw a terrapin in the yard that was in real bad shape. He was moving slowly and I saw that his shell was all busted up—must have been hit by a car or something. Anyhow, I saw that he needed a repair job so I went into the house and got a roll of silver color duct tape and the scissors. I put him on the work table in the wood yard and taped his shell back together. Made a pretty neat job and told him to stay away from the road and he probably would be safe. With that bright silver tape, he would be highly visible. I will be able to see him when I am cutting grass. I don't know where he went. I saw him a few times since, wandering around in the back yard. He really appreciated the repair job, but didn't have Medicare so won't be able to pay."

After reading a "100 Years Ago" item, Nip recalled some "good old days" in his own life. He remembered when he had a Texaco station in Memphis in 1937, there were three gas pumps. The lowest grade was called Economy and the gas was colored purple. It sold for 16 cents a gallon. Regular was Fire Chief and was 18 cents. The top grade was Sky Chief and sold for 22 cents.

Nip also remembered early Sunday morning haircuts when he was a child. The four older boys went together with Robert taking care of the money--$1.00 for the four haircuts. The barber was Mr. Ford Moore. Later, when Nip was in California, he found most haircuts there were a quarter.

Nip usually bought gasoline at "Get-N-Go" in Viola. On one occasion he checked to be sure he had sufficient money in his wallet before going to the station. He had $21—a twenty-dollar bill and a one-dollar bill. He felt that was sufficient and planned to stop putting in gas at $20; however, he wasn't quick enough, and went eight cents over $20.

He went inside and gave the cashier his $21. He knew it was not unusual to be given back a few pennies in change, but he was surprised that she rang up $20 and returned the one-dollar bill. When he emptied his pockets that night, he found the cashier had not returned the one-dollar bill, but mistakenly had given him a ten-dollar bill. He had put it into his pocket without looking at it closely. After pondering what to do, he phoned the station and asked for the mailing address. He wrote a check for $9.08 and mailed it to the station with a note. He explained he was returning the $10, less the eight cents he owed for the gas, and less the one dollar he should have received instead of the $10 bill. "I didn't lose any sleep over it. No guilty feeling, and I do not want what is not mine."

Chapter 19
Time for Change

After getting the propane heater in his kitchen, Nip's tree-cutting and wood-chopping chores lessened considerably; however he still had to maintain a supply of wood for the living room heater. He wrote, "I have been lucky to have a lot of favorable weather to cut trees and get enough wood in to keep the living room heater fired 24 hours a day. By using short wood and keeping the fire in the back of the stove, I can keep the ashes raked to the front and can shovel them out without letting the fire go out."

During the winter of 2000, when the temperature was about 9°, the propane tank sprang a leak. For some time Nip had been considering buying his own tank and using a different supplier; however, when he called the company from which he rented the tank and reported the leak, a repairman came immediately. The response was so quick, he began to rethink the idea of changing to another company, even though he could buy gas for quite a bit less from a supplier whom Marty had recommended.

Shortly before Christmas Nip had another problem. During a heavy rain, his roof began leaking. There was no way to put buckets under all the leaks in the living room ceiling. He moved everything except the couch and one lamp into another room until repairs could be made.

It was the worst winter Nip had experienced since moving to Arkansas. Ice covered the roads and only those with four-wheel drive were able to leave their homes.

"I thank God for the wonderful neighbors. They are all ready to come to my aid—the Bridges family, the Dillingers, Matt (the mailman) or Rick Foster." He was not left out of Christmas meals and family celebrations even though he couldn't drive on the ice. His neighbors came for him and took him back home with food to keep him eating for days.

In order to keep the fire burning in the living room stove, Nip had to add wood three times during the night. He would set an alarm clock and sleep on his back, with a hearing aid in his clock-side ear. When the alarm rang, he hurriedly added wood, reset the alarm, and quickly got back under the electric blanket.

Afraid that Nip would fall on the ice, Tom Bridges bought him a set of spikes for his shoes. Although he didn't like having to take them off when coming inside the house, Nip said they were wonderful and allowed him to walk to the mailbox and woodshed.

The weather continued to be extremely cold during the coming month, with several of his neighbors losing cattle. Tired of being housebound, at first opportunity Nip headed for Salem. He reported buying six loaves of bread, even though he had three in his freezer, because it was on sale, three loaves for $1.00. He also went to the courthouse to pay his personal property tax. The only thing listed was his 1970 Ford pickup truck, valued at $50!

Although he fretted and worried about his utility bill being high, Nip kept an electric heater on in his cellar during the freezing weather to protect his pump and water pipes. Additionally, an electric fan blew heat from the kitchen stove to pipes underneath the house. His pipes didn't freeze; however, there were a few times that he skipped his scheduled Monday wash day, finding that the old wringer washer worked equally well on Tuesday or Wednesday. When the weather was extremely cold, he found it was all right to skip a week or two.

Nip was shocked when he got his 2001 tax bill—not larger, but smaller. He felt there had been an error and he made a quick visit to the assessor's office. "I didn't want to later learn my property was being sold because of unpaid taxes." He was assured no mistake had been made. The Arkansas Homestead Act took effect January 1, 2001, and real estate taxes were repealed. Thereafter, his tax payment was slightly more than $4.00 annually.

Whether or not Nip was allergic to the pneumonia shot as he claimed, he certainly was very sick that spring and was moved from the Fulton County Hospital in Salem to Mountain Home, where he was hospitalized and under the care of a lung specialist. Nip thought he surely was going to die at that time and said he always had wondered how it was going to be in his last days. I told him I felt he was going to live for quite some time, even though I too had doubts. With Felix also sick, I could not stay full time with Nip when he was released from the hospital. I made arrangements for him to enter the small nursing home operated by Mary Jane Foster. She and her husband Loyal were friends of Nip, living less than two miles from his house. Although Mary Jane had facilities for only six, she recently had lost one patient and fortunately had a room for Nip. He received the best of care but felt uncomfortable as the only male resident. He was eager to be back in his own house and was able to do so after two weeks of Mary Jane's special care. This move would have been impossible without the extra attention provided by his gracious neighbors.

Before many weeks, Nip was back on his riding mower cutting grass, but he realized he no longer had the strength and energy to cut trees and keep wood for the living room stove. It was time to have another propane heater installed. Although he had considered a heater similar to the one in his kitchen, he learned the radiant-type wall heater would cost much less and would operate more efficiently. He had one installed in his living room before the end of summer.

Although Judy Dillinger had begun doing laundry for Nip during his illness, when he recovered, he again filled the washing machine and rinse tubs and did his Monday wash-day job. This was something he really enjoyed—that and his riding mower, and he devoted a great deal of time to taking care of Muffin. "I cut grass all morning and would have cut more this evening, but had to cook and bone chicken for the dog. I told her to go easy on the chicken as they haven't had a 39-

cent sale in quite a while and 49 cents is too high. It comes in 10-pound packages."

While Nip was in the hospital he had gotten several bedsores, which Mary Jane had treated when he was under her care. Several months after he was back in his own house, one spot still had not healed. It took some "sisterly insistence" before he would inform Dr. Phillips about the sore and allow her to look at it. To his dismay, she arranged for Home Health nurses to make regular visits and redress what he referred to as his "sore butt." Dr. Phillips also made arrangements for oxygen to be delivered to Nip and his nightly use of oxygen continued throughout the rest of his life.

Even though Nip thought highly of Dr. Phillips and usually accepted all her recommendations, there was one he refused. She suggested he begin participating in "Meals on Wheels." This went no further than the initial visit by local representatives. They questioned whether or not he had stocks and/or bonds, and he said he did not. One of the visitors then said it was understood he had CDs and asked what was the total of this investment. "I just sat there and looked at her. I never answered. Then the bombshell! She said, 'Mr. Hall, would you say that you have in the neighborhood of $100,000 in CDs?' I then spoke. I said, 'Lady, I don't know where you got such ideas or information of this sort, but even if it was true, I would not verify it, and I am not answering any of your questions. I am not interested in Meals on Wheels!' She thought that over a bit and then said she would leave her card in case I changed my mind. She told me their meals were well received and the cost to me of $4.25 was more reasonable than any I could get at local restaurants or cafes and would be delivered right to my door. She put her card on my little table and left. I expect the price of those meals is based on a personal financial worth. I am not having any. The TV dinners suit me fine and even when they are not on sale, they are well worth the price."

Nip loved to "poor mouth" and would lay it on thick at every opportunity, especially in regards to his prescriptions. On a visit to the clinic in Salem, Dr. Phillips asked if he had any questions. "I said yes, a few, and first, did she think it was necessary for me to keep the appointment with Dr. Galli in Mountain Home? She said yes, that he needed to see if there was any change in my lungs and that was his specialty. Then I asked how many prescriptions I could discontinue. I said I have already cut down on some and I was intending to cut some more or drop them. I said I think I am taking too many pills and tablets—14 a day, and they are expensive. I said I spent $284 on pills last month. She said some might be reduced, but all medicine is outrageously high these days. I said I agree, but I am wondering if I need all this amount of medicine and anyhow my budget is being stretched past the limit. Everything is costing more and my income is less every month. I said, as you know, my only income is my Social Security check of $369 per month. I showed her a maturity notice from the bank, showing interest on a CD had dropped from 6.5% to 3.5%. I said when your income is cut about half, you just have to do some adjusting—either cut bread or pills, and I have just about decided I would rather have bread."

After his pitiful story, Dr. Phillips looked over this list of medications and marked out a couple and reduced several, but reminded him that he must realize he needed everything that could be done to combat pneumonia. She stressed that at his age, pneumonia often is fatal.

Although he survived pneumonia, he complained that it took him longer to take care of necessary chores. He made two important decisions. First, he decided there was too much grass for him to cut. Marty Dillinger agreed to rent most of his property, including the orchard, and fence it as pasture for his cattle. Nip retained only a few acres close around his house, garage, workshop and sheds. He was able to keep this area mowed and trimmed. The agreement was good for both parties.

The other big decision required much more consideration. AmeriGas, from which he rented a tank and bought propane, had given him good service and was quick to respond whenever he called. By mid-summer 2002, however, that company was charging $1.10 per gallon. He learned he could purchase a 500-gallon tank from Anderson's, another supplier, for $895. The first fill would cost only 49 cents per gallon, with a guarantee of 69 cents for one year. The total for the purchase of a new 500-gallon tank, including installation and 400 gallons of propane would be $1,197.07. Nip notified AmeriGas to pick up the rented tank, and the company reimbursed him for the propane it contained. He made a good change and always was pleased with the price and service from Anderson's.

Marty had told Nip he would uncover the turbine "whirly" on his roof. Marty got busy and the weather got hot, so Nip climbed a ladder and uncovered it himself. When he told Judy to let Marty know he had done it, she fussed, saying he could have fallen. Nip said,

"No chance. Believe in the Word of God. Isaiah 42:6."

Nip also believed in helping his neighbors, who so often came to his aid. He noticed that although the Dillingers' yard had been mowed, no trimming had been done. He knew at that time neither Walter nor Judy were physically able to handle their weed-eater, and their sons were spending many hours in the hay fields. Nip saw this as an opportunity to return the many favors he had received. Using his own weed-eater, he worked two days, several hours at a time. His neighbors protested, but he proved to be willing and able to take care of their needed trim work. He told them he was old and slow, and had to rest a lot, but was happy he could help.

Going to the Dillingers' house for Sunday night supper became routine for Nip and was a pleasure he looked forward to and seldom missed. He often had a Biblical question with which to challenge Brother Michael and they had many thought-provoking conversations. Nip went with Judy and Walter to Michael's church in Pomona, Mo., several times, but was embarrassed because he could not hear well.

Nip enjoyed hearing Michael tell about a wedding he conducted. The groom had worn a roping outfit, complete with cowboy boots and western-style hat. The bride was attired in a gingham dress and old-fashioned hat, and was barefoot! After they repeated the marriage vows, the groom added, "I love you and we will share almost everything, but I also love my Harley motorcycle, and it will still be mine— not ours!"

After Nip had his 90th birthday, he quit driving, saying he realized his reflexes were not what they ought to be and he did not want to risk having an accident, possibly injuring others as well as himself. Thereafter he depended on his neighbors when transportation was needed. This primarily involved trips to Salem for appointments with Dr. Phillips, banking, a stop at Dollar General for Muffin's dry dog food and a few other items, and shopping at the Town and Country Grocery for "TV dinners," several loaves of bread, and a 10-pound pack of chicken legs and thighs to be cooked for Muffin. The highlight of almost every trip was a hamburger, fries and drink at Sonic.

Nip kept his pickup truck in the garage, occasionally starting it and backing down the driveway to keep the battery charged. Although he had said that after his death the truck was to be given to Walter Dillinger, he wanted it in his own garage until that time came.

One trip Nip no longer had to make was to the barbershop. Either Marty or Charlotte kept Nip's hair trimmed, and on one occasion, he did a fair job himself.

Charlotte accepted the responsibility of keeping up with all of Nip's prescriptions, picking up his medications at the pharmacy, and filling his pillboxes every week with the pills and tablets he should take over each seven-day period.

As Nip's energy waned, filling the wash and rinse tubs became a thing of the past. Judy regularly took care of Nip's laundry. Not only did she take his clothes and linens back clean and neatly folded, she returned everything to the right drawer or shelf and it was not unusual for her to replace worn items.

As Nip often said, no one had better neighbors!

Chapter 20
Remembering

As Nip's physical activities decreased, or went into a slower mode, his mental condition seemed to never falter. He did a lot of "recollecting" and shared these thoughts verbally or in his many letters.

Our father dug and repaired wells and Nip recalled the time a new well was needed for their own home. Nip and his older brothers told Daddy about a man who claimed he could find the best place to dig for water by "water witching," which involved the use of a forked switch (small branch from a tree). "Daddy just laughed and said it was really stupid and he would prove there was nothing to that tale. He cut a limb with a nice handy 'fork' in it from a peach tree and started walking back and forth from our old bucket-and-rope well on the west side of the house, all around down along where the well was to be dug. When he got to a certain spot, he said the dowsing fork turned in his hand and he could not hold it. He told us boys that spot supposedly was where water could be found, probably at about 60 feet (the depth of the old well) and said for us to start digging. He would not even help drill the well. Robert, Norris, Adam and I, and two Negro boys, George and Russell Ford, got to work. At 35 feet we struck water that gushed almost to the surface. Robert installed the strainer, cylinder, etc., and we pumped it clear and called Daddy. He just couldn't believe it and it bothered him. He never tried water-witching again and wouldn't talk about it.

"Well, there sure was plenty of water there as was proven when the corn crib burned. I was the one delegated to keep that gasoline engine running at full speed, holding the throttle open for half a day. The well never ran out of water. Dad lost nearly 1,000 bushels of corn. The smoke was seen for miles and miles. People came from as far as Mississippi to see what was burning. The smoke sure was billowing. Afterwards Dad built a new barn on the same spot, this time using corrugated sheet metal instead of wood."

Nip said questions he received in letters from niece Da (Dorothy Faye), our sister's oldest daughter, often kindled memories of incidents he had not thought about in 50 or 60 years. (Da is a very talented artist and wrote her Uncle Nip many letters. He especially enjoyed her beautifully painted cards.)

Before our grandmother, Eva Pauline Little, married our grandfather, Richard Robert Redford Hall, she had divorced an abusive husband, James Baxter Davies. An item in "Old Shelby County," a Memphis newsletter, about Davies Manor in Brunswick brought further memories to Nip.

"I have seen Davies Manor when we had the store in Brunswick. I think Ellen Davies Rodgers probably was a member of the Brunswick Garden Club. She was in Brunswick a number of times. I don't know whether you knew it or not, but Hillman Rodgers (Ellen Davies' husband), as a favor to Daddy, used to bring him $50 in coins and small bills to the curb market every Saturday morning for their change box. He would come by Saturday afternoon and pick up his $50. He worked for the Tayloe Paper Company, and Daddy bought all the paper bags and paper cartons, etc. from them."

Back to current events: On a trip to the grocery with Charlotte, Nip found bread on sale at 19 cents, with a two-loaf limit. They each bought two loaves and when they loaded the groceries into Charlotte's jeep, she put one of hers in with his groceries. When they got to his house, he said he owed her for the bread. Charlotte said, "You have got that all wrong. I owe you. You have spoiled my kids with candy and cookies, and you have taught them to think of someone beside themselves. When only one of them is with me, you always insist they take the same amount of candy, or whatever, to the other one. That is something they had never done before." Nip enjoyed the children in both the Bridges and Dillinger families, and they filled an empty spot in his life.

Visiting with Nip a short time later, Charlotte said she wanted to thank him for "getting Bailey straightened out." Nip was puzzled, not remembering anything he had done or said. Charlotte reminded him that Bailey had been pouting and had been angry with her on their last visit. She said after he talked to Bailey, she got over her "mad spell" and behaved. As Nip later recalled, "I told Bailey the Bible says you must honor your father and your mother so that you will have a long life, and I want to add that I sure hate to see you mad at your mother because there is going to come a time when you no longer have a mother or a father. That isn't maybe, it is a fact, and then it will be too late to be sorry."

A few weeks after Nip celebrated his 90th birthday, Judy took him for an appointment at the Ozark Eye Center in Mountain Home. Nip had been told several years earlier he had cataracts, but there was no need for surgery at that time. Prior to each visit, Nip would remark that he probably would have one cataract removed while at the center. He understood this to be minor surgery and thought one cataract would be removed while he was there for his checkup and in a couple of weeks, he would return to have the other one removed. This never happened. On each visit he was told there was little change in his eyes over the previous year and cataract surgery was not necessary.

Soon after his eye examination in Mountain Home, Nip made an appointment with Dr. Totter, optometrist, who had a once-a-week office in Salem, to see if he needed new glasses. Dr. Totter assured Nip his eyes had not changed since his present glasses were made. He saw no need for Nip to order new glasses, as they would not improve his eyesight. Nip accepted this second opinion and decided he was blessed to be 90 years old and able to read and watch television—without cataract surgery or new glasses! It was his night "vision" that had him puzzled.

"I woke up suddenly about 2:30 a.m., I believe it was, and I heard someone talking. I do not wear my hearing aids at night, so could not have actually heard by ear. Anyhow, the voice was in the room, and I was awake. I thought I recognized the voice, but I asked, 'Who are you?' I was really scared to move. He said, 'You know this is Buff.'

"I said, 'I know it is not Buff.' He said, 'Well, if you are so sure, just why don't you turn on your nightlight? I dare you to.' Well, I did just that. I turned on the nightlight. There was nobody there but me. So I still wonder how you can have a vivid dream (?) when you are wide awake, even carrying on a conversation."

A few weeks after Nip's "night vision," he shared another of his unusual experiences.

"I went out on the back porch to get something out of the freezer compartment of the refrigerator. I had put some ice cream in there, and I noticed it had completely melted. When I checked, I discovered everything had thawed. The bread I keep in there was just like when I had put it in there several days before. I checked the refrigerator to see if it was cold. Actually, I couldn't really tell as the temperature on the back porch was around 35° or so, which would be as cold as the refrigerator should be. I opened the kitchen door and fanned some warm air into the refrigerator and it kicked on and ran about five seconds. The freezer part never got any of the refrigeration, as I held my hand over the coil and it never changed."

The nearest Whirlpool authorized repairman was in Cherokee Village. After discussing the situation with Walter Dillinger, Nip decided rather than getting his 18-year-old refrigerator repaired, it would be more practical to purchase a new one. Judy told him she would be taking daughter Sheila to West Plains to look at freezers and invited him to go with them the next day. Nip said he would be ready.

"Well, that night I went to bed and then at 12:00 midnight I woke up with a bang! Something said to me, 'You do not need a new refrigerator. There is nothing wrong with the one you have.' I said, 'Oh, yes, there is. It is not working.' The voice said, 'You need to get the freezer part going.' I said, 'How?' The only answer I got was 'A'. That was all—no more. I thought maybe I would know more the next morning and I went back to sleep.

"The next morning I went out and looked inside both compartments. I looked at the temperature controls—there were two, one for the freezer and one for the refrigerator. Each little wheel had an arrow on the side for colder or warmer. I got my flashlight, as the wheels were small with just the rims showing.

Well, the refrigerator had numbers and it was set on number three. I looked closely at the freezer control and faintly saw a 'B' and I figured there must be an 'A' too. The control was stuck and probably had not been moved in 18 years. I finally loosened it and turned it to the 'A.'

"I thought I had the answer, but to be sure, I put a pan of water in the freezer and in a couple hours it was frozen solid.

"When Judy came the next day and asked if I was ready, I told her I wasn't going. I said everything was fine. She asked who had fixed it. I told her I did as I was told to do and that was all there was to it. She said, 'Mr. Hall, who told you what was wrong with that refrigerator?' I said, 'Well, when you really can't find the answer to a problem, there is The One up above who knows all the answers!' That's all I ever told her."

A few weeks later, although the freezer part was working, the refrigerator part quit cooling. That was not a major problem as he still had a small refrigerator they had discontinued using when they bought the larger one. "I just plugged in the little one and put all the stuff in it. There was plenty of room—just a matter of correct placing, and it sure beats that big one. It got cold in a hurry.

Still set on three, just like we used to use it. The only thing is that it is not a self-defrost, but it uses about one-half the amount of electricity as the big one. I think I will just forget about getting a new one. I already like the old model better." He later said evidently he had misunderstood the earlier 'message' about the old refrigerator and probably it was meant as a warning of what was coming!

Nip often complained about the large amount of mail he received from charitable organizations seeking donations. (Actually, he enjoyed getting mail regardless of what kind it might be!) He said the mail deliverer probably thought he was a millionaire from all the solicitations he got. Some he supported; others he pitched.

Nip thought he had the phone callers figured out. He would not answer until after the third ring. He said if the phone rang as many as four times, he would answer. Because solicitors do not want to waste a call on a recorder, Nip said they would hang up if no one answered after three rings. There were a few times when his method failed and he would pretend he thought he was being offered assistance. He would explain he was elderly, with limited income, and would appreciate any help that could be given to him. There would be a quick disconnect.

Sometimes he answered a "wrong number" call he enjoyed, although he would never admit it. "I got a phone call this evening from some man. He asked if Cecil was home, I said I didn't know because I didn't know where Cecil lives. He asked if this was 458-2630. I said yes, and the only one living here is myself, Frank Hall, and Muffin, and Muffin is not here at the present. She probably is out chasing a squirrel or something, as she is my dog. He said he was sorry to have bothered me, but someone had given him the wrong number. I said that's OK. I hope you find Cecil."

Before Nip ate his own breakfast every morning, he fixed breakfast for Muffin. When he called and she came from her bed in the garage, he wished her a good morning, petted her and stayed while she ate. If she didn't come immediately, he usually would take her bowl back into the house before birds, squirrels or 'possums ate her food. Wild turkeys (that were not very wild) also liked Muffin's dog food. One day he heard Muffin barking and looked out to see a big 'possum attempting to get to the porch. "Muffin kept blocking it. Every time Muffin would get real close, it would turn to face her, but Muffin was quick to move. I knew if it ever got a chance, it would kill Muffin. It had a mouth like an alligator, with rows of about two-inch teeth, sharp as needles, and the mouth was open wide, ready to eat a small dog. I tried to run it off, but that just got Muffin more excited, so I gave up and told Muffin 'OK, but you ought to know you can't whip that one.' I went back into the house and looked out every now and then. Muffin had sort of cut down on the barking. The critter was still out there, watching from beside the walk, but Muffin was staying on the porch, guarding the steps. Before I went to bed I took Muffin's pan in. She was still there, but the critter was gone. I guess it gave up, but I have decided to bring in Muffin's pan every night whether it is empty or not."

The phone rang early on a Sunday morning. Nip answered, feeling it would not be a call from a charitable organization on Sunday. He was surprised the call was from the Town & Country grocery store in Salem. He was told the store owed him $6.00 and he could stop by the office next time he was there and get the money. "She said the last time I was there, a week ago, I had written a check for $6.00 more than the bill and the checker failed to give me change. I thanked her, but could not figure out how that had happened. I dug in the trash box and found the old cash register tape. It had a total of $13.95. Then I looked in my checkbook and there it was—Town & Country, $19.95! I guess I misunderstood the checker and thought he said $19.95. He didn't look at the check and rang up $13.95, the correct total. The office must have found the register was $6.00 over and traced it down. There still are plenty of honest people in this world. (Also deaf ones!) I thought that was pretty good detective work, locating the one who had overpaid a bill."

Chapter 21
When Someone Cares

With a distance of 200 miles between Viola and Memphis, where most of Nip's relatives lived, family visits were always cherished. Nip had a special relationship with Bobby Hall, son of brother Robert, because they shared the same birthday—October 10, born exactly 30 years apart! (Also birthday of Susan Hoover, who faithfully remembered her "birthday twin.")

A few months before their 2004 birthday, Bobby and friend Polly spent a Sunday afternoon with Nip. They listened to his stories, looked through photo albums, toured the orchard, and then took him to Sonic in Salem for his "usual"—burger, fries and cola. Nip explained he was borderline diabetic and a Coke or Pepsi was a special treat. At home usually he drank artificially sweetened Kool-Aid. His favorite flavor was pineapple, but he had not been able to find it for a long time. A few days later he was surprised when Matt, the mail carrier, delivered a package from Bobby— 15 packets of pineapple Kool-Aid. Bobby said he wanted to send an entire case, but that was all he could find.

One day following a summer shower, Nip felt the ground was dry enough for him to tie two bags of empty cans onto his riding tractor-lawn mower and head for the "dump" at the back of his property. He rode near enough to toss the cans into the landfill, but when he tried turning the tractor around, the wheels mired into the ground. "The more I worked with it, the worse things got. I cleared all the big rocks out of the way, but still could not go anywhere except the wrong way. I finally had gotten really dug in, with the rear wheels both sunk to the axle. I decided the only way I was going to get out was to walk back to the house and get my come-along and some heavy rope and chains I had used to pull down trees when they wanted to fall the wrong say. Then I thought, I just can't carry all that stuff all the way back down here. I just gave it a real good thinking-over. Then I said, 'Will I ever learn? All I have to do is ask and I will be shown.' So I did just that. I prayed. I said, 'Lord, I need help. I am asking you to show me how to get this thing out of here and back to the house.' Well, right away I saw a small post that Marty had left, so I went and got it. I said, 'Now, what next?' Rocks everywhere. So I got the idea. I piled up a couple bushels of rocks near the back wheels and then stuck the post under the axle. With my foot I started shoving rocks under the wheels. I kept at it until I got each back wheel about six inches above ground level, then tapered down in front of each wheel. I said, 'Lord, I am ready to run in home now.' I got on that joker, set it in third gear, throttle wide open, came off that ramp I had built, and zoomed up the hill, kicking rocks the size of baseballs all the way."

Nip's property was a safe haven for wildlife. One morning he counted 19 wild turkeys in his front yard. Nearly every day deer were seen in the orchard. They seemed to prefer pears to other fruit and they were fond of almonds. Occasionally one ventured to the front yard, but Muffin was quick to scare it away.

At one of the Salem stores an employee asked Nip if he wanted to live to be 100. "I said it didn't matter to me, one way or the other. I am ready to go or to live. When you get old as I am, it just isn't important as long as you are not a burden for anyone. I have lived a good life and have made my share of mistakes and errors of judgment like everyone else. Sometimes I wonder just why I am still alive.

Only God has the answer. It must be I am still needed for something."

Nip's hearing worsened as he aged and he kept trying new hearing aids—the mail order kind! He said new ones cost less than having old ones repaired. "The one I bought last January is the best one I ever had, so I decided to get another one while they are available. They also are the lowest priced ones. I have over a dozen, but most need some kind of repairs. They all ask for $85 in advance for repair work, then parts and labor. 90-day warranty. Just not worth it for three months, and this company admits that about half sent in for repairs only need cleaning, which is impossible for the owner to do as they have to be taken apart to be cleaned"

Nip's 91st birthday was celebrated "big time." Charlotte, Bailey and Roy took a complete dinner to his house, along with a chocolate birthday cake. He appreciated the presents, including a soft pillow, but it was the gift watch he found fascinating. "It has the day of the week, date, time, and other buttons to push for daylight savings time, and even a button to push to light it up for night."

He also had a birthday celebration with the Dillingers. "As usual, they had an enormous feast and I went home with enough food for several meals, including half of an angel food cake, strawberries with whipped cream, and pie with artificial sweetener." He appreciated Judy's birthday present—10 microwave dinners! (Nip referred to them as "TV dinners" and he stocked up when they were on sale.)

A trip to Salem with Charlotte included his buying "a few items at Dollar General and quite a few groceries at Town & Country: 12 TV dinners at 69 cents each and 10 pounds of chicken legs at 29 cents per pound, five loaves of bread, milk, dry cereal, etc." (I had urged him to keep a good supply of food and other items so as not to impose upon his neighbors for trips to Salem. He took me at my word!)

Back at home from Salem, Nip put away the groceries while Charlotte removed his window air conditioner so he could cover the outside panes with plastic for the winter months. He then shared a letter from me with an e-mail message from Da (niece Dorothy Faye), advising their daughter-in-law's cancer had worsened and she was critically ill. "Charlotte said we would have to do some real earnest praying. I said I also will call the team (Prayer Power Club) and Monday morning there will be over 5,000 prayers going up for Janice, at 9:45 a.m., and I will be one of the 5,000."

(Bit of trivia: Nip said Charlotte's name officially is Charolette and is so spelled on her birth certificate. Since this is not a familiar name to most people, she decided to "go with the flow and be Charlotte" except when the correct name is necessary.)

Nip admitted to having been careless on the riding mower. He rode too close to a bush and a low-hanging branch stabbed his hand. When he was able to get the bleeding stopped, he applied an antibiotic ointment and bandaged it well. "Then I gave thanks that it was already healing."

According to Nip, Judy prepared an all-time feast for Thanksgiving Day, and he ate too much of just about everything he was not supposed to eat! Additionally, she sent him home with three trays of food, including six kinds of pie. "I was determined to eat all I could hold and to enjoy it, as I said it could be my last. Everything in our lives comes to an end sooner or later—sooner for us oldies!" (His report from the clinic the day before Thanksgiving was not good. He had lost five pounds since his last visit and had fluid on his lungs, causing him to be very short of breath.)

The next few weeks brought snow and ice. Nip ventured outside no farther than the front porch to feed Muffin, now leaving her bed in the garage only to eat and drink. He was more concerned about her comfort than his own. She, like him, was getting old. She no longer jumped up onto the porch, but would come up the steps slowly when he whistled for her.

As the Christmas holidays approached, Nip tried to capture the spirit of the season but confessed his inability to keep up with all the ongoing activities. As in years past, I did his shopping early, delivering the presents for neighboring families to his house weeks before Christmas. I could not take the chance that snow or ice might prevent travel later in December. Together we examined every present, especially those for the children, to be sure he was pleased with the gifts I had purchased. After all were gift-wrapped, he stashed them away in his back bedroom and put a "Do Not Enter" sign on the door. It was such a pleasure for him to be able to give Christmas presents to those who gave so much to him throughout the year.

Working for the school system gave Charlotte time off during the holidays. She knew Nip was not feeling well and her daily visits to check on him were interspersed with phone calls. Less than a week before Christmas she took him to the clinic, and Dr. Phillips prescribed a new medicine. After two days on the medication, he awoke feeling extremely dizzy. "I almost blacked out. I got to the kitchen and my vision was going away—getting dimmer and dimmer. I turned around and headed back to the living room, picked up the phone and got into the recliner. About that time Charlotte came in and asked if I was all right. I said I wasn't sure. She and Tom were on their way to get a load of wood as they were almost out. Tom had been sick and needed her to help, but she said for me to keep the phone with me and to call them on Tom's cell phone if I needed them."

Nip didn't know if the dizziness was caused by the new medicine he was taking or because the previous day he had forgotten to take his morning pills. He always took most of his daily medicine at breakfast, and he did not realize he had missed taking any of it, including the new prescription, until the next day.

Soon after Charlotte and Tom left, Judy came with enough food for several meals. While she was there, Charlotte phoned twice and talked with her about their plans for Christmas. They both were concerned about Nip, and with several inches of snow on the ground and his feeling dizzy, they felt he should not try to leave his house. Charlotte said she would celebrate with him on Christmas Eve.

"I had Christmas dinner here at home with Charlotte, Bailey and Roy. Charlotte brought the dinner and presents and we had a real good time. After dinner Bailey washed the dishes and cleaned up everything and put the left-overs in the refrigerator. While we talked, Charlotte fixed my pills and said I needed a haircut. I said OK and she cut my hair. We opened Christmas presents. I had presents from Bailey and from Charlotte and Tom. I already had gotten presents from Tri-County Supply and from Matt and Tina Hart (mail carrier). This was Christmas Eve. Charlotte was going to have Christmas Day dinner with her Mom and Dad."

The Dillingers came for Nip on Christmas Day and he celebrated with that family, including children and grandchildren. He again had a tremendous meal, enjoyed the fellowship, and returned home with trays of food and an armload of presents.

"This has been a really good Christmas." Wonderful neighbors made it happen!

Although the weather improved during the last days of December, Nip's health continued to decline. "I have been having too many Happy Holiday celebrations, with too much forbidden food! Oh, well, Christmas comes only once a year and you only live one life here on earth!"

Chapter 22
The Year 2005

As the new year began, Nip's dizzy spells became more frequent and more intense. Dr. Phillips had taken time off during the holidays to be with her family, and Nip was anxiously waiting for an appointment as soon as she was back in the clinic.

"I do not like this vertigo or dizzy feeling I have every day. Anytime I stand, after sitting a while, I almost black out. Tim (the pharmacist) said I should talk with Dr. Phillips about trying a different prescription. I most surely will do it. I think it bothers Charlotte worse than it does me. She keeps a close check every day—sometimes two or three times a day. I have tried the oxygen right after I get up, but all that did was give me a lot of twisted tubing to recoil. It didn't help whatsoever. It just doesn't pay to get old!"

On his first January visit, Dr. Phillips found his blood pressure to be low and advised him to discontinue blood pressure medication and not to resume taking it until his blood pressure reached at least 130/60. She stressed that at his age it would be even better if it were about 165/65.

I was able to take him for his February appointment with Dr. Phillips. His blood pressure still was low. Nip thought his old monitor might not be accurate so he purchased a new one that slipped onto his wrist. With the press of one button, it gave a reading that also included date and time—in large red letters, and stored the data for a maximum of 100 readings.

Omitting blood pressure medication did not eliminate Nip's dizziness. In mid-March he had a severe spell. "Every time I got up onto my feet, I would start to black out. Everything would get darker and darker and I could barely see across the room. I had to sit down or fall down—not much choice there so I chose to sit."

He called the clinic and found Dr. Phillips would see him, although he did not have an appointment. The problem came with finding transportation. He first phoned Phyllis Coggins, who took care of his oxygen. Many times she had told him to call her for anything he needed. This time she was sick in bed with flu. He tried to reach Marty, but he either was asleep or outside. He knew Judy was working. Walter, now sheriff, was on the job in Salem and had some prisoners he could not leave. He dialed Charlotte's office number and was told she was attending a meeting in Salem. He was trying to decide whom to call next when Sheila (Dillingers' daughter) walked in with Raven, her little girl. Walter had gotten in touch with her. Nip was glad to hear her say, "I've come to take you to the clinic."

They arrived shortly before noon and were there until almost 4:00 p.m. Once again Dr. Phillips said Nip's blood pressure was low. She instructed him to stop all medication except Dioxin, to closely monitor his blood pressure and return in one week.

By the end of March Nip was feeling somewhat better and had started doing a bit of outside work. "I am not making much progress. Every time I start to do one thing, something more important pops up and I get sidetracked. I am still in the process of getting the yards in shape to start mowing the grass. Yesterday I was going to get out the riding mower and trailer and pick up more limbs and some rocks. There seems to be more rocks than ever. The varmints dig them up. I just happened to check the oil in the tractor and it was very low and black, so I decided I'd better change the oil first. But then when I turned around, I noticed that the ground wire to the power plant was broken loose at ground level. This being a dangerous situation if I forgot to fix it, I knew I had better take care of that first. The wire was too short to reach the outside spike, so I had to find a suitable piece of wire.

"Well, after I got that done, I got ready to get the tractor out to change the oil. The battery was low and it wouldn't start. No trouble, I thought. I got my big charger out and discovered the rats or squirrels had chewed the insulation off, about four feet from the end. This part would be lying on the ground and possibly short out, so I needed to tape it—each wire separately. I didn't have any friction tape, so I temporarily taped it with paper masking tape. By that time, I had decided I needed a snack and a drink of water, so I headed for the house.

"I am slow and tire easily so after a snack, I sat down for a few minutes' relaxation. I got in the recliner and flipped on the TV to see if anything was going on. Before I knew it, I had dozed off, and the few minutes actually had turned out to be about an hour. Oh well, at my age, there is no rush. Anyhow, Muffin was having a time trying to show me how hungry she was, so I said 'All right, I'll feed you,' and I did. Then I decided it just wasn't my day for working outside. I went back and gathered up my tools and junk, closed the door on the fix-it shop, and said tomorrow is a new day."

Nip had planned to buy some friction tape on his next trip to Salem so he could replace the temporary masking tape on the wires to his battery charger. "This brings up another of His mysterious ways. When I was in Salem, I had the tape on my list. I buy such as that at Dollar General, but they had every other kind of tape. No friction tape. I said that was no problem because I would get some at Town & Country. They always have such items. They also were out. I asked one of the stock boys. He looked and said it seemed to be the one item missing. Yesterday evening, for no reason at all, I happened to open the door to the old, big refrigerator. The only item in there was a two-roll pack of electrical tape, probably been in there a year or more. I don't remember having put anything in that refrigerator. You see, I was prevented from buying the tape because I did not need it!"

It was obvious Nip's health was rapidly deteriorating. Judy and Charlotte made frequent visits, usually with plates of food. After learning Nip had taken a tumble down his front steps, Marty put up a handrail for him. He no longer made daily walks to the mailbox. With a letter from Dr. Phillips verifying Nip's condition, Matt Hart, the mail carrier, was given permission to make door delivery. Matt, a long-time friend, did even more. Every day he stopped at the road, walked to the house, put Nip's mail on the cabinet just inside the front door and took any outgoing mail. This gave Matt an opportunity to check on his neighbor and he did so faithfully.

My trips to Viola were more frequent, always taking an ice chest of homemade soup, stews and other foods that were quick and easy for him to warm in the microwave. I drove over to see him on May 3 and stayed overnight. We talked about his condition. "Walter said I probably will live to be 100, but you and I know that's not so. I just hate leaving so much for you to take care of when I'm gone." I assured him I knew what he wanted done and I would carry out his wishes to the best of my ability.

The next morning after breakfast I told Nip I needed to go to Mountain Home. I didn't tell him why I was going because I knew he would say the trip was not necessary. However, he needed a new microwave. He had bought, or been given, pot pies in microwave-safe bowls, which he saved, thinking they were reusable. He learned he was mistaken when he attempted to use one and it exploded. The inside of the microwave was blackened and marred. I was appalled that he was still using it and attempted to convince him it was unsafe. My first purchase in Mountain Home was a new microwave oven.

A five-gallon gas can was next on my shopping list. Nip was anxious to begin cutting grass again, but was concerned because he did not have gas for the mower. He said in the past when he needed gas, he had siphoned it from his truck. Since he no longer drove, he would ask one of his neighbors to drive his truck to the station and fill the tank. I said he should not be siphoning gas and assured him I would get gas for his mower before I went home. Then I found he only had one-gallon gas cans! Returning from Mountain Home, with a new five-gallon can, I stopped at "Get-and-Go" in Viola and bought gas for his mower.

On Saturday, May 7, Nip went to a birthday party at Marty and Amy's house. "I am not sure which of the kids had a birthday. It looked like all celebrated equally. I ate too much, as usual, and also ate things I shouldn't eat. Michael said he was glad to see that I was blessed with such a long and healthy life. I said 'Well, I sometimes wonder if it is such a blessing to live to such an old age.'

"I'll write you another letter in a few days and continue this one. (I hope!)"

That letter never came. After several days without hearing from him, I phoned Charlotte. She confirmed what I felt—that he probably did not feel like writing. Our niece Virginia (Cholly) went with me to Nip's on May 24. He wanted to go to Dollar General and to the grocery store (to buy chicken for Muffin). Wearing house shoes to Salem was a first for Nip, an indicator of how bad he felt. It was sad to watch as he shuffled along, holding onto the shopping cart. He did not want to stop at Sonic for his usual hamburger, fries and cola—another first. He did, however, eat well that evening after resting in his recliner.

The next morning Cholly and I continued house-cleaning as Nip watched from his recliner, which was not really *his*. Charlotte had felt he needed something more comfortable than the couch. Not only could he lie back and relax in a recliner, but also it could be placed near the heater. Charlotte and Tom had moved it from their house as a gift to him.

Nip questioned Cholly about her age, saying he noticed for the first time she had gray hair! When she told him how old she was, he shook his head and said, "I must really be getting ancient!"

Every year as winter approached, Nip covered his windows on the outside with plastic to keep out the cold air. He surprised Cholly and me that day by saying he was not going to do that any more. "I'll just burn as much propane as it takes to stay warm." We agreed that was a good plan.

We said our good-byes and were walking toward the door to leave when Nip said he wanted me to do one more thing. He told me to phone Anderson's and ask the price of prepaid propane. Although he had bought nearly 200 gallons less than two weeks earlier, he wanted his tank completely filled. Delivery of 400 gallons was made the next day.

Charlotte took Nip to Salem for an appointment with Dr. Phillips on June 1. After examining him, Dr. Phillips said he needed treatment at the hospital. Charlotte took him to the Fulton County Hospital. After several hours he was discharged and Charlotte took him home. He phoned me that night. He sounded weak and our conversation was short. "They really worked me over at the hospital."

The following evening, June 2, Charlotte saw lights on in his house as she drove past. Since it was later than his usual bedtime, she went back to see about him. He was in the recliner, weak but conscious. Unable to get him onto his feet without help, Charlotte phoned the Dillingers. Walter came immediately and they stopped for Judy en route to the hospital. Fortunately, Dr. Phillips was on duty at the hospital that night.

Felix and I were away from home when Charlotte phoned about 10:00 p.m. to tell us they were taking Nip to the hospital. Thirty minutes later, as I was listening to her earlier recorded message, Charlotte called again and said he was very ill. I couldn't drive that far at night, but said I would be on my way at daybreak. Her final call came just minutes past 1:00 a.m. Dr. Phillips stayed with him the entire time, as did Charlotte and Judy, and I was assured he died peacefully and without pain. Although I was not there, it was comforting to me to know these three ladies, whom he loved and respected, were at his side. These and other neighbors helped me over the next seven days in more ways than can be imagined.

Visitation was arranged for Sunday afternoon, June 2, at the Cox-Blevins Funeral Home in Salem. As Nip had requested, the funeral service on the afternoon of June 3, was conducted by Brother Michael Dillinger. My son Gary Wagoner sang "Angels' Band," playing his guitar as accompaniment. I thanked the many friends who came to pay their last respect to my brother. He was buried in Mt. Calm Cemetery next to his beloved Hazel.

Family members later gathered at Nip's house to share a bountiful meal prepared by friends and neighbors, whose kindness and support had made it possible for him to live those final years where he wanted to be—in his own home on Brentwood Lane, Viola, Arkansas.

"It is great to have friends when one is young, but indeed it is still more so when you are getting old." — Edvard Grieg